"*Adult AD/HD* is a must-read for adults with AD/HD and those who love them. Whether you read this book from cover to cover, skip around, or skim the 'just the facts' boxes, you will come away with a wealth of information, strategies, hope, and inspiration."
—**Wendy Richardson**, M.A., MFI, author of *The Link Between ADD & Addiction: Getting the Help You Deserve*

"The premiere do-it-yourself book for adults with AD/HD. Concise, factual, and highly readable. This is a book you can skim—but don't!"
—**Stephen C. Copps**, M.D., director, Central Georgia Institute for Developmental Medicine; author of *The Attending Physician*

"*Adult AD/HD* picks up where other books about AD/HD leave off, providing much-needed help and hope for adults in a field that is dominated by literature about children. Novotni and Whiteman offer practical ideas about how to live with AD/HD in the world of work, relationships, and adult responsibilities. Simply put, *Adult AD/HD* is the best book for adults who have or think they might have an attention disorder that I have read."
—**Bob Seay**, web editor, *ADDitude Magazine*, additude.com

"Public understanding of AD/HD in adulthood has increased dramatically over the past decade, thanks in part to books such as *Adult AD/HD*. Michele Novotni and Thomas Whiteman have written a reader-friendly, insightful, warm, and practical book. I recommend it highly for all adults with AD/HD and those who love them."
—**Peter Jaksa**, Ph.D., former president, Attention Deficit Disorder Association

A Reader Friendly Guide to
Identifying, Understanding, and Treating
Adult Attention Deficit/Hyperactivity Disorder

Adult AD/HD

Thomas A. Whiteman, Ph.D.
Michele Novotni, Ph.D.

WITH RANDY PETERSEN

P.O. Box 35007, Colorado Springs, Colorado 80935

OUR GUARANTEE TO YOU

We believe so strongly in the message of our books that we are making this quality guarantee to you. If for any reason you are disappointed with the content of this book, return the title page to us with your name and address and we will refund to you the list price of the book. To help us serve you better, please briefly describe why you were disappointed. Mail your refund request to: Piñon Press, P.O. Box 35007, Colorado Springs, CO 80935.

© 1995, 2003 by Michele Novotni and Thomas Whiteman

All rights reserved. With the exception of page 71 and pages 268-272 as specified on pages 267 and 271, no part of this publication may be reproduced in any form without written permission from Piñon Press, P.O. Box 35007, Colorado Springs, CO 80935. www.pinon.org

ISBN 1-57683-357-7

Cover design: David Carlson
Cover illustration: Dolores Fairman
Interior illustrations: Marty Dundics
Creative team: Nanci McAlister, Greg Clouse, Darla Hightower, Glynese Northam

Some of the anecdotal illustrations in this book are true to life and are included with the permission of the persons involved. All other illustrations are composites of real situations, and any resemblance to people living or dead is coincidental.

This publication is designed to provide accurate and authoritative information in regard to the subject matter covered. It is sold with the understanding that the author and the publisher are not engaged in rendering legal, accounting, or other professional service. If legal advice or other expert assistance is required, the services of a competent professional person should be sought. From a Declaration of Principles jointly adopted by a Committee of the American Bar Association and a Committee of Publishers.

Novotni, Michele.
  Adult AD/HD : a reader friendly guide to identifying, understanding, and treating adult attention deficit/hyperactivity disorder / Michele Novotni, Thomas A. Whiteman, with Randy Petersen.
      p. cm.
Includes bibliographical references and index.
  ISBN 1-57683-357-7
  1. Attention-deficit disorder in adults--Popular works. I. Title: Adult attention deficit/hyperactivity disorder. II. Whiteman, Tom. III. Petersen, Randy. IV. Title.
  RC394.A85 N678 2002
  616.85'89--dc21
                                                2002012420

Printed in the United States of America
1 2 3 4 5 6 7 8 9 10 11 12 / 09 08 07 06 05 04 03 02

CONTENTS

ACKNOWLEDGMENTS

We would like to acknowledge the following colleagues for their help with this project.

Stephen Copps, M.D.—Provided review and insights for the chapter on medication.

John Thomas, M.D.—Provided medical management and consultation for many of our AD/HD clients and also provided insights for the chapter on medication.

Edna Copeland, Ph.D.—Provided insights for the assessment chapter.

Bill Morgan, Psy.D.—Provided much of the material for the chapter on behavior modification and shared his insights and stories.

John Taylor, Ph.D.—Provided research and insights on nutrition for the alternative treatments chapter.

Sharon Mathias—Gathered data, tracked down leads, and helped us coordinate the many meetings necessary for a project like this.

To each of these people we extend a heartfelt thank-you. Your work was well above the call of duty!

AN INTRODUCTION

THERE ARE SILENT STRUGGLES THAT GO UNNOTICED BY THE general public. These battles are waged in the lives of people who have AD/HD—Attention Deficit/Hyperactivity Disorder (formerly known as ADD). They are among the most misunderstood people in the world.

Sometimes they're considered dumb because they forget things or have lapses in concentration—but they're not dumb.

Sometimes they're considered rude because they blurt out inappropriate statements at inopportune times—but they're not trying to offend anyone.

Sometimes people get frustrated with them because they seem to have great potential but they never seem to live up to it. Yet no one is more frustrated than the people with AD/HD themselves.

We have talked with thousands of people who have AD/HD. It has touched our own families, our own lives. We share in the struggle. We hope this book will promote understanding, inspiration, and practical help to many who struggle with AD/HD and to the many who care about them.

READER-FRIENDLY FORMAT

This book is written in a style that works with people who have attentional difficulties. We've learned that people with AD/HD often start books but don't finish them. So, our first goal is to make it highly readable for those who are easily distracted. But don't let that fool you. If you're looking for scholarly research and serious treatment, it's in here!

Adult AD/HD is still pretty new. Only recently have professionals begun to identify it. In fact, there's still some confusion over the name and the different forms it takes, especially in adults. We will tell you what the experts say and what they suspect. We will also give you real-life stories of people who share your struggles.

The format of this book may take some getting used to. To make it more reader-friendly, we're putting all stories and illustrations in italics. If you get bogged down in stories and want "just the facts," skip the story sections. If you love stories and need examples to keep you interested, zoom ahead to those if the text gets dry.

We also provide summaries at the end of each chapter. It's common for people with AD/HD to sometimes read a page or two and then forget what they just read. The chapter summaries will give you quick takes on the material. And the index at the end of the book will help you quickly find topics you are seeking.

CONFRONTING THE CONTROVERSY

Controversy still surrounds AD/HD. Sometimes it has seemed like the "Disorder of the Month," with everybody claiming to have AD/HD and using it as an excuse for poor work and bad manners. Others still deny the existence of AD/HD. Treatment recommendations vary widely and cause many with AD/HD to go into a tailspin. In our first section, "Living with AD/HD," we will help you separate facts from fiction so you can make informed choices that work for you.

In our second section, "Getting the Right Diagnosis," we will examine proper diagnostic methods. Who is qualified to diagnose and treat AD/HD? Are there any recognized tests for this disorder?

Just what are the symptoms of AD/HD? They can be quite confusing. How can so many different symptoms be connected with the same disorder? In our third section, "Recognizing the Symptoms," we'll talk about what AD/HD looks like. You may see your own reflection in that part of the book.

How should AD/HD be treated? Some try stimulants; others try behavior modification methods or therapy. Do these things work? Should you seek medication or meditation? There are drugs that lessen the effects of AD/HD, but aren't there some cautions involved? And what is the role of counseling in all this? In our fourth section, "Exploring Treatment Options," we'll review the many treatment methods available.

Finally, our fifth section, "Overcoming AD/HD Difficulties," focuses on the problems faced by the person with AD/HD. With any treatment method, there are still life issues that you have to deal with—rocky relationships, challenges on the job, continuing organizational and learning difficulties. We offer specific strategies for success in each area.

IT'S NOT CALLED ADD ANYMORE

People often talk about ADD (Attention Deficit Disorder). In fact, an earlier version of this book was called *Adult ADD*. Now we're calling it AD/HD (Attention Deficit/ Hyperactivity Disorder). Is this something different? No, only the name has changed.

Sometimes teachers or writers or your next-door neighbors will still use the term ADD, and that's fine. It's easy to understand, and it rolls smoothly off the tongue. ADD is even seen in the names of some great support organizations for folks who have it. But the official term that the medical community has chosen is AD/HD, so that's what we'll use.

I WONDER WHAT THEY ARE GONNA CALL IT NEXT YEAR!

ABOUT US

Both of us, Michele and Tom, are licensed psychologists in southeastern Pennsylvania. Michele Novotni is in private practice at the Wayne Counseling Center, Wayne, Pennsylvania. She is the author of *What Does Everybody Else Know That I Don't? Social Skills Help for Adults with AD/HD* and *The Novotni Social Skills Checklist.* A columnist for *ADDitude Magazine,* editor of *FOCUS Magazine,* and president of the National Attention Deficit Disorder Association (ADDA) Board, Michele also travels throughout the world speaking on topics related to AD/HD. This has become a specialty of Michele's because her father and one of her sons both have AD/HD.

Tom Whiteman, who has a moderate form of AD/HD himself, has also conducted seminars on adult AD/HD in the Philadelphia area with overwhelming response. Founder of Life Counseling Services of Paoli, Pennsylvania, Tom has considerable experience treating childhood AD/HD, especially during his eight years as a school psychologist in the Philadelphia School District.

Between us, we have seen thousands of clients learn to manage their AD/HD using one or another of the methods we describe. There is certainly hope and help for those with AD/HD!

As you read, you should know that we are using real stories in this book. We have gained permission from a few clients with AD/HD to tell their stories and to use their names. We are grateful to Maria Bassler and Helen and Laura Thompson. They all felt strongly that there was no reason to be ashamed of AD/HD, and so they agreed to be interviewed for this book, letting us use their names and their stories.

In many other cases, however, to protect the privacy of the people mentioned, we have changed names or minor details, but the stories are true.

If you have AD/HD, think you might have it, or know someone who might have it, you've come to the right place. Read this book in your way, at your own pace. But please read it. You should find information, tips, and encouragement that will help.

PART ONE

LIVING WITH AD/HD

CHAPTER ONE

NAMING THE BEAST

A MAN COMES HOME FROM WORK, PICKS UP THE MAIL, TURNS ON the evening news, and starts opening his mail as he half-listens to the TV. Then he remembers that he had to call his office to leave a message for the office manager. He drops the mail between the cushions of the sofa and heads for the phone in the kitchen.

When he gets to the kitchen he sees the refrigerator and feels hungry. He pokes around the fridge and makes a snack. With the food, he heads back to the family room to watch TV, completely forgetting about his phone call.

Later that night he asks his wife if she has seen the mail. "I haven't seen it," she says, and he becomes angry with her.

When she conducts a search and finds the mail in the cushions of the sofa, he sheepishly apologizes. "I guess I just forgot about it. Sorry."

Does this scenario sound familiar? Scenes like this replay themselves daily in the lives of people with Attention Deficit/Hyperactivity Disorder (AD/HD). Long considered merely a childhood problem, AD/HD is now being recognized in a growing number of adults.

The mail-in-the-sofa story seems harmless enough. But what about that call the man forgot to make? What if it was crucial for a major business deal? The man might find himself without a job.

What if the mail contained an important document and was lost for days instead of hours? What if the flare-up at his wife was the ninth one that week and the marriage was already in trouble?

It's no joke. People with AD/HD can find themselves unemployed or underemployed because they cannot consistently focus on their responsibilities. Their finances may be in shambles. Their relationships are often rocky.

Maybe you already know the story.

How Many of These Statements Sound Like You?

"I set things down and forget where I put them."

"I start projects but have difficulty following through."

"I find myself jumping from thing to thing."

"I have difficulty concentrating."

"My life is fairly disorganized."

"I've had difficulty working up to my potential."

"Sometimes I say or do things without thinking."

"I feel misunderstood by others."

A WORLD OF HURT

For Michael* (all names followed by an asterisk have been changed), forgetfulness and a lack of organization have been hallmarks of his life. Though he is really quite intelligent, he always had difficulty in school. He found ways of scraping through high school and he even tried going to college, but he struggled with most of his classes.

Michael managed to work in various jobs while he finished up his college degree at night. Now he works as a salesman and spends a lot of time on the road in dialogue with his clients. He is able to make a decent living doing this, and it is by far the best job he has ever had. It is also the longest he has ever worked at the same job—eight years.

The recurrent problem in his job is his disorganized style and forgetfulness. Frequently he is late for appointments, but with a car phone he can overcome most of the fallout from this trait. He is almost always late with his paperwork and mileage reimbursements.

At first Michael's boss and his secretary had fits with his habits, but now they overlook his faults because he makes up for it in sales. He is very good with people—outgoing and friendly. His clients like having him stop by and are happy to give him orders. (If only he could get them in promptly, he wouldn't have to make excuses about how "the office messed up their order.")

Michael's marriage has been a similar series of frustrations, except his wife is much less forgiving. After all, she has to live with him! "He's always jumping from thing to thing, and never completes anything!" Peggy exclaims in frustration.

They have been married now for eighteen years and have two children. When the children were young, things *were at their worst. Peggy almost left Michael because of his lack of help around the house. At one point she felt she couldn't even trust him to watch the kids while she went out. Oh, Michael would intend to be a good baby-sitter, but then he'd pop a video in the VCR and go off to read* Field and Stream *magazine, eventually forgetting all about the kids.*

Finally Michael and Peggy reached a truce as Peggy gave up trying to change him. She began to expect less and less from him, but she wondered what happened to that charming, intelligent young man she thought she had married.

This is an uneasy peace, however, as there are weekly, sometimes daily, flare-ups. Peggy has very little patience for his forgetfulness or excuses. She interprets his behavior as being deliberately resistant. Michael is also frustrated with his inability to please her. He wants to, but he just can't.

AD/HD is often misunderstood. The intelligence of children with AD/HD is often underestimated. AD/HD children can gain a reputation as difficult because they don't remember a teacher's instructions, can't concentrate on the subject matter, or can't sit still.

The same misunderstandings can carry into adulthood. People with AD/HD can seem rude or ignorant, lazy or rowdy. Often it's assumed that someone with AD/HD is hiding some deep rebellion, and chronic lateness or lack of discipline is seen as a passive-aggressive way of taking revenge.

But people with AD/HD are as frustrated with their problems as those around them.

Gifts and Limitations

Amy* is a very successful businesswoman, with her own marketing agency and eighteen employees. I (Tom) went to her office for consultation about marketing a new service we wanted to provide to the community. As I sat in the waiting room, glancing through a magazine and listening to the soothing music, I almost nodded off.

Then the whirlwind hit.

A woman dressed in blue jeans and a pullover sweatshirt whooshed into the lobby and all of the staff snapped to attention. She handed out orders—"Type this. Take care of that for me. Have this mailed out right away." The staff moved quickly to do her bidding.

"And where's my eleven o'clock appointment?" she barked.

I snapped to attention. "I guess that would be me."

As we headed to her office, she pelted me with questions. But before I could finish an answer, she was asking the next question. And once we were in her office, I saw how Amy lived. There was a computer covered with papers. A bulletin board with loads of memos attached. She had a radio on an all-news station providing background noise the whole time we talked. But the most annoying part of the conversation was the way she would ask me a question and then look over my head as I spoke.

This was so annoying that I actually turned around and looked behind me. There was a TV set on with the sound turned down. Amy mentioned that she watches the financial news and keeps an eye on the ticker all day long.

After she asked about my project, I began to interview her. Sensing her hyperactivity, I began to ask about her work style, her relationships, and her personal life. She had always excelled in creative areas, she told me, but lagged behind in academic subjects. After college, she had taken jobs wherever she could get them but was very frustrated in each one. She described herself as being way ahead of most of her bosses—something they never seemed to appreciate. Finally, Amy found a boss who really appreciated her style. She found people around her who could make up for her weaknesses.

Amy's big break came when one of her biggest clients offered to help her start her own agency. Now she enjoys running her own show. "I need at least three people running around behind me, following through on all my ideas," Amy proclaimed. "I know I tend to drive people crazy, but I have good ideas, and I'm most productive when I'm freed up to do what I do best—dream and create."

Amy's personal life is not nearly as successful as her professional life. While she is in her mid-thirties, she has not had a serious relationship since college. "Men are intimidated by my success," she explained.

I encouraged Amy to look at her own distractibility and the fact that she is pulled in so many directions. "How can you carry on a serious relationship if you can't direct time and energy into making one thing work well and follow through on what you commit to doing?"

That's when Amy opened up. She admitted that she's fine on the first few dates. She has lots of fun because she has so many diverse interests—museums, theater, golf, tennis, hiking. She enjoys many things. Men love that.

But when it comes to following through on her commitments, or when the relationship requires a focused conversation or working together on shared goals and objectives— well, Amy finds that much more difficult.

"That's why I have an office staff," she explained. "They

handle the details for me. It works in business, but it's murder in a relationship."

Hyperactivity is often, but not always, associated with AD/HD. Folks with AD/HD often feel a need to be doing five things at once. They may tend to work best with a radio going and perhaps a TV on. And, with the right support system, they can be very productive.

Such people can also be extremely creative and very outgoing. Their high energy tends to be attractive (but sometimes tiring). Often they'll have many friends but few deep relationships. Amy's story is not unusual in that respect. High energy can get you through the first few dates, but when it's time to hold a real conversation, things get tough.

FAKING IT

Aaron's* life has been a series of failures. It all started in school with constant efforts to get passing grades while feeling stupid and out of touch. While others were learning and progressing in school, Aaron felt frustrated and humiliated by his inability to pick up even the most basic skills.

Early in life, Aaron learned how to fake it. He nodded agreement when he wasn't sure what the teacher was talking about. He pretended to know how to read when he wasn't sure of the words. He actually made it through high school by faking, avoiding, and—when he had to—cheating. He graduated with only an elementary level in reading and math, even though others considered him to be of average ability.

After high school, Aaron got a job in a gas station. His parents urged him to go to college, but he put them off by saying that the gas station job was just temporary, a way of saving money for school. But in truth, Aaron did not believe he had the ability for college. He felt like a fake and was more comfortable in a setting where there were few challenges.

At work Aaron was gaining more and more responsibilities. He had a good way with people but didn't understand many basic concepts. He would use his learned coping skill—faking it—whenever he had to do a cash deposit or read anything of substance. The owner, however, was impressed with his work and began to trust him more and more.

Still filled with self-doubts and personal insecurities, Aaron became night manager, which gave him two new responsibilities. He had to keep track of a lot of cash, and he was sent out to do towing jobs several times a week. Both turned out to be big problems.

Aaron had difficulty totaling the cash and filling out the deposit slips. He was afraid he would show everybody just how incapable he was. So he began to drink heavily—a six-pack of beer each night. It was Aaron's way of self-medicating his low self-image and personal pain. He assumed no one would notice if he began pocketing cash from the station. It was an easy way to pay for the beer.

So Aaron would hang around the station drinking and then get a call for towing. Fortunately his drunk driving didn't result in any accidents. But finally he got caught driving under the influence of alcohol. Aaron lost his driver's license and then lost his job.

The court ordered him to see an addictions counselor, who treated him for alcoholism. In gathering Aaron's history, the counselor also asked about his educational and learning problems. It was apparent that these were at the root of his low self-image, self-doubts, and feelings of inadequacy. Drinking *was Aaron's way of numbing the pain of feeling stupid. He considered himself a disappointment to his parents, his friends, and to himself. A six-pack would help him forget all that for a few hours.*

As it turned out, Aaron was referred for further evaluation and was diagnosed with AD/HD. He was able to receive treatment, but that's not an automatic happy ending. There was still a lot of damage to repair. He had to get honest about the things he had never learned when he was faking it in school. Now Aaron is taking some remedial classes at night school. He and his parents are hoping he can eventually take college courses or technical training in order to get a better job.

The Common Thread

At first glance, Michael, Amy, and Aaron seem like totally different people with totally different problems. One is a forgetful, disorganized, middle-level management man; another is a highly successful, hyperactive woman; a third is a young man who has experienced a series of failures, including a drinking problem. Yet each of them has been diagnosed with adult Attention Deficit/Hyperactivity Disorder.

How can one disorder apply to so many situations?

Perhaps Michael is merely forgetful or sloppy. There are lots of people like that in the world, right? Maybe Amy just drinks too much coffee. And how many people like Aaron could we find—slow learners with drinking problems? It seems too easy to call all of this AD/HD.

Isn't this just another of those self-help gimmicks, the issue of the month, a subject for the next TV movie? Are we merely giving Michael an excuse he can tell his wife? Aren't we just giving Amy a reason to feel she has overcome something? Maybe this diagnosis gives Aaron some hope, but is there any substance to it?

Even though professionals have been treating adult AD/HD for well over a decade, there is still some skepticism about its diagnosis. Is it really that much of a problem, some wonder, or just a short attention span? But when you meet Michael, Amy, Aaron, or a hundred other people with AD/HD, this theoretical issue suddenly becomes real. These are people who don't always fit in. Their minds work in a different way. In some cases, their lives are falling apart because they cannot focus consistently like "normal" people do. It is not just lack of discipline. It is not just sloppiness. It is not just a free spirit. There is a problem that holds these people back. It's as real as a broken arm, but much less obvious.

Attention Deficit/Hyperactivity Disorder has been recognized in children for more than a hundred years. Often associated with hyperactivity, AD/HD first appeared to be something that kids outgrew as they entered adulthood. But then the experts started finding adults with some of the same AD/HD behavior—lots of them. They weren't running around rooms like hyperactive youngsters, but they were tapping and fidgeting.

The scientific research on the subject of adult AD/HD is fairly new. Yet we know there is a physical aspect to the disorder—an imbalance that affects the brain's ability to process information (more on this research later). And there are medications that can make up for this imbalance. So AD/HD is not just "all in your head"—well, it is in your head, but not just in your imagination.

So how can you tell if you have AD/HD? That's where it gets confusing. Here is a partial listing of the possible symptoms of AD/HD:

- ▶ Forgetfulness
- ▶ Difficulty focusing on any one task
- ▶ Difficulty following conversations, particularly when there are several people involved
- ▶ Tendency to take on too many projects and then not finish most of them
- ▶ Time-management problems
- ▶ Easily frustrated
- ▶ Frequent moves or job changes
- ▶ Pattern of underachievement or underemployment
- ▶ Difficulties with relationships
- ▶ Tendency toward substance abuse
- ▶ Low self-image or insecurity at approaching new tasks
- ▶ Impulsive decision-making style
- ▶ Tendency to take risks
- ▶ Not sticking with long-term projects
- ▶ Tendency not to read or finish books (magazine or newspaper articles preferred)
- ▶ Not understanding social nuances
- ▶ Difficulty with paperwork (getting things in on time)
- ▶ Difficulty managing finances and checkbook

Another area is especially significant: People with AD/HD often lack insight into how others perceive them. In other words, you may think you're fine, but you might be driving other people crazy in some of these areas. So, before you rule out any of these symptoms, check the list with someone close to you.

IS THIS FOR REAL?

Probably everyone in the world can relate to at least some of the characteristics listed here. And remember that this is a *partial* listing. One article reviewed the literature and found a total of sixty-nine symptoms and thirty-eight causes cited.[1]

So how do we figure out who has AD/HD and who doesn't? Professional organizations are developing guidelines for assessment that are readily available on their websites.[2] There are various screening tests available (and we'll present you with a preliminary screening test in this book), but these tests differ in their breadth. After initial screenings, brain scans are beginning to be used to assess AD/HD, but the interpretation of this data is still controversial.

Some experts consider AD/HD quite rare, afflicting less than 2 percent of the public. Others say that one in five people may have AD/HD. We suspect there is a large group of people with "mild AD/HD," exhibiting some of the symptoms but experiencing only minor difficulty in their lives.

AD/HD is a real problem, affecting real people. Let's all be careful how we use the term and not fall into the trap of attaching the AD/HD label to just any dysfunction or difficulty. AD/HD appears to be a many-headed beast. It takes many forms, but there are common threads of causes and symptoms. Once we accurately name a problem, we can know better how to deal with it.

There's a curious reaction among those we have diagnosed with AD/HD. Yes, as you would expect, some of them worry about what's wrong with their brains. But for many it's an "Aha!" moment. There is relief and even joy as they realize their lifelong problems do not stem from laziness, stupidity, or selfishness but from a brain-based difficulty. It's AD/HD.

And once we name the beast, we can tame it.

Just the Facts

- AD/HD takes different forms—difficulties staying focused, disorganization, impulsivity, creative hyperactivity, or general underachievement, to name a few.
- We should all be careful about overdiagnosing and underdiagnosing this problem.
- Though it may be a "fashionable" problem to have these days, that does not negate the fact that some people really do have it and it affects their lives greatly.

NOTES

1. Gay Goodman and Mary Jo Poillion, "ADD: Acronym for Any Dysfunction or Difficulty," *Journal of Special Education* 26 (1992), pp. 37-56.
2. *www.chadd.org; www.add.org.*

CHAPTER TWO

BEYOND THE BLAME GAME

DIANE* HAD A PROBLEM. HER AD/HD SYMPTOMS WERE AFFECTING *her work and she was on the verge of being fired. Her greatest difficulty was in prioritizing her tasks; she tended to major on the minors.*

Through counseling, she determined to make a last-ditch effort to communicate with her boss about her problems. She did not make demands but suggested certain ways the boss could help her be a better worker. (Her counselor helped her devise these ideas.)

First, she asked if she could meet with the boss for a few minutes at the start of each day to go over her list of things to do. The boss would identify the most important projects for her to tackle. Diane also asked for "time spacing" on her monthly reports—intermediate deadlines in mid-month. Previously, she had waited until the last minute to prepare these, but now she asked her boss to hold her accountable to those earlier deadlines.

Diane also asked for a flex-time arrangement. She knew she had to be there for most of the working day, but she got her best work done when no one else was around. The boss agreed to let her come to work an hour-and-a-half late and stay an hour-and-a-half late, so she could have that prime time at the end of her working day. In fact, the boss agreed to all her suggestions. He had to spend a few extra minutes with her, but he got a much more effective employee out of this arrangement.

Too many companies have a business-as-usual approach. Despite legal requirements, they are relatively inflexible to the special needs of certain employees, such as those with AD/HD. But increasingly, businesses are realizing that people with AD/HD (and others) have a lot to offer, and a few minor adjustments could pay off in the long run. Diane's boss realized this, and it resulted in a win-win situation.

But Diane's attitude was important, too. She was not blaming anyone. She was offering her best efforts and suggesting some new arrangements. Unfortunately, some others are taking very different approaches.

THE EXCUSE

When Frank* was first diagnosed with AD/HD, he became very emotional. He felt as if twenty-some years of pain were being released at one time.

In school he had thought he was stupid because he had a lot of difficulty keeping up with the classes. Then he thought he was unemployable as he moved from job to job. Then, through a period of unemployment, he fought feelings of laziness. Finally, he got a sales job that he seemed to do well with, but he had a very difficult time getting along with his boss.

Frank also had trouble in his marriage. His wife labeled him "passive-aggressive." Whenever he was late, forgetful, or insensitive, she assumed he knew exactly what he was doing and did spiteful things just to upset her.

Then Frank heard a radio show about AD/HD. He made an appointment with the doctor who had been on the radio and was diagnosed. He had AD/HD.

Years of failure and frustration were all explained away in one brief evaluation! Now he had a reason for the way he acted!

This would be a wonderful success story if it weren't for the fact that now Frank had more than an explanation—he had an excuse.

He told his boss he couldn't be expected to sit through staff meetings. He claimed that he couldn't do any of his paperwork, and whenever his sales figures dropped, he blamed it on AD/HD.

His marriage went from bad to worse. All those times his wife accused him of being passive-aggressive—well, now he knew he was falsely accused. And she still didn't fully understand how "handicapped" he really was. He now had an excuse for being habitually late, for not following conversations, for being insensitive, and for not being able to follow through on household tasks or chores. His wife would give him lists, which he would usually ignore. After all, he was AD/HD and couldn't be expected to remember such lists.

Some people who have AD/HD have used the diagnosis as an excuse for irresponsible behavior. They use it at home, on the job, anywhere they might have responsibilities they'd like to avoid. They use AD/HD as a license to be self-centered. They make no effort to change.

We're treading a fine line here. AD/HD may explain a person's irresponsible behavior, but it doesn't excuse it. It

LIVING WITH AD/HD

is very difficult to live with AD/HD. Those who grow up with it face years of low self-image, frustration, and impaired achievement. They tend to be chronic under-achievers, yet most of them find ways to cope with it. They learn to excel in certain areas. Having AD/HD might be a legitimate explanation for why a person struggles at certain tasks, but it is not an excuse to stop trying to manage the symptoms or to accept less than one's best.

One man, an executive in a publishing company, bemoaned the day an employee was diagnosed with AD/HD. "He had been a fairly good worker," the boss reported. "He didn't really excel at his job, except for the fact that everyone liked him. He was a real people person. And he was steady. He wasn't very fast at any of the clerical skills necessary for his job, but he plugged away."

One day the employee announced that he had been diagnosed with AD/HD. The boss was skeptical at first, because he had never suspected that the employee had any kind of disability. He had always seemed "normal" to him.

The employee explained, however, that he couldn't do more than one thing at a time, and that he needed a private office with a door, and that he couldn't handle the phones if they interrupted his concentration. "I tried to accommodate him," the boss said, "thinking it would be worth it if it helped him to work faster. But the opposite happened. He did less and complained more."

Soon the demands grew. The employee couldn't have any talking outside his office. Then no one was to interrupt him when the door was shut. The whole company tried to play by his rules, but still his productivity decreased steadily.

"He always had excuses for why he couldn't get any of his

▼

projects done," the boss said. "Finally, I had to ask myself, 'What am I paying him for? I have an employee here who needs a private office with no interruptions and no phone calls, and he still can't get his work done. I don't even afford myself those kinds of luxuries, and I'm the boss!' I had to let him go."

What was causing the problem here? AD/HD? Not really. The employee had AD/HD all his life, but he was doing an acceptable job before his diagnosis. What changed? His attitude. Once he knew he had AD/HD, he began to use it as an excuse. He began to focus on his rights as a victim of this disorder, not on his responsibilities as an employee of this company.

We don't mean to minimize the difficulty this man was facing. But it seems as if he stopped trying as hard once he was diagnosed with AD/HD. Having AD/HD is not an excuse to avoid work. The diagnosis should instead motivate those with AD/HD to learn all they can to overcome its effects.

YOUR RESPONSIBILITY

If you have AD/HD, you have a responsibility to "manage" it. That means controlling your behavior. In mild cases of AD/HD, you may be able to manage it through counseling, behavior management, coaching, and sheer determination (with help from family and/or friends). In severe and moderate cases, you would probably benefit from medication and counseling.

In every weakness there is strength. This is true of AD/HD as well. For all of the negatives, there are also positive aspects. Find your positives and capitalize on them. Are you creative, fun to be with, friendly, exciting, smart? Then put yourself in positions where those qualities can come out. As much as you can, avoid situations that require the abilities in which you are weak. Try not to take on tasks you know you won't complete. Try to avoid overwhelming projects or extremely distracting environments. This is all part of managing your AD/HD. Know your strengths and weaknesses, and lead with your assets.

Vicki*, a woman with AD/HD, came to me (Tom) for a career assessment. She was frustrated with her job and was looking for a new direction. As we examined her strengths, we found creativity, people skills, and an ability to communicate and persuade others. She particularly liked to be outside. She liked to have a variety of tasks. She enjoyed moving about.

Yet Vicki found herself in a job where she sat at a desk all day, rarely moved from her chair, and had very little contact with other people. She had no outlet for her creativity; she was just expected to follow the routine. No wonder she was looking for a change!

I recommended a job as a salesperson, one where she would be on the road, making decisions, on the move, meeting with people. As it turned out, Vicki got work selling medical supplies to physicians' offices. She is well-liked, does quite well, and loves her job. Her clients look forward to her visits.

Vicki was not playing the blame game. She could have demanded that her previous employer make major changes to accommodate her. If she was then fired, she could have hired a lawyer to sue for damages under the Americans with Disabilities Act. She could have used her AD/HD as an excuse. Instead she used it as a springboard.

Just the Facts

- ► Some use AD/HD as an excuse for inconsiderate behavior, causing difficulty in their relationships.
- ► While society should be sensitive to the special needs of a person with AD/HD, those with AD/HD bear responsibility for their own actions.
- ► People with AD/HD have a responsibility to "manage" their AD/HD and to seek treatment.
- ► Many people with AD/HD strive day by day to succeed in a difficult world, without making excuses. We applaud them.

PART TWO

GETTING THE RIGHT
DIAGNOSIS

CHAPTER THREE

Is it AD/HD—or Isn't it?

ADULT AD/HD WAS AN ALMOST UNKNOWN SYNDROME TWENTY years ago. Professionals were trained to think that attention deficits and hyperactivity only existed in children, and the effects wore off or "matured" sometime in adolescence. This gave hope to many parents.

Yet I (Tom) noticed something unusual about many of the parents I was telling this to. They seemed different. Not necessarily hyper, but different in a similar way to their kids. Some were distracted, jumping impulsively from subject to subject. Others would relate to my explanation of their children's symptoms by saying, "I understand; I was the exact same way when I was in school." They complained of continuing problems with reading, spelling, and (most commonly) organizing their lives. The apple doesn't fall far from the tree, I reasoned. I did not know of any official research to back me up, but it wouldn't have surprised me to find that these parents had an adult version of AD/HD.

My casual observations were borne out in research literature that spread into the national spotlight in the mid-1980s. Apparently other people had noticed AD/HD symptoms in adults. Some researchers were suggesting that there was such a thing as adult AD/HD, that children did not always outgrow it. For some time it was a matter of debate among mental health professionals. But now there is a growing body of research indicating that adult AD/HD not only exists, it is treatable.[1]

With the diagnosis and treatment of this "new" disorder, many have found relief from lifelong symptoms that have deeply affected their careers, their relationships, and their lives.

I became even more aware of the issue when I left the school setting and entered a private practice to counsel adults. Many clients with histories of learning problems were having extreme difficulties with their relationships and on their jobs. Could this be adult AD/HD? But how could so many be afflicted with a disorder that was unknown a decade earlier?

Then a local newspaper was preparing a story on adult AD/HD. The reporter called my colleague (and coauthor), Michele Novotni, for some quotes. Her name appeared in the story, and within days our counseling center had more than 150 phone calls from people asking to be evaluated for this syndrome. We had hit a sensitive nerve.

A few of the callers were obviously just overreacting to the media hype. But most of them had valid concerns. They had at least some of the symptoms of AD/HD and wanted to know if this could be the reason they had so many problems in their marriage or on the job.

For many, the answer was yes. But not everyone who is distracted at work has AD/HD. If you find it hard to follow conversations or if you struggle with remembering certain kinds of information, it doesn't necessarily mean you have AD/HD. Sometimes it's just a personality quirk or a lack of discipline or a crowded schedule. Sometimes there's another psychological issue involved.

As it turned out, some of our 150 callers did not have AD/HD. Some had different problems that we could help with. Yet for many others, that phone call was the first step in a life-changing process of diagnosing and treating the disorder that had plagued them for years.

Jason* first came to our counseling center after hearing from a friend that we diagnosed and treated adult AD/HD. He had been diagnosed as manic-depressive several years earlier and had since been taking medication. Then he started hearing and reading about AD/HD.

As he read stories of other distraught and even depressed people who were misdiagnosed by other psychologists, Jason latched onto the idea that this was his case. When he brought this up with his own doctor, the doctor barely acknowledged Jason's concerns. Now he was in my (Tom's) office, convinced that his real problem was AD/HD—not depression. He wanted me to help him stop his medication for depression and start him on his new treatment plan for AD/HD.

This is a common problem and one of the reasons adult AD/HD has been so controversial. As we consider Jason's situation, we need to keep two things in mind.

1. The diagnosis of AD/HD is very complex. The symptoms can be similar to other emotional conditions (such as depression). Therefore, while many would want to self-diagnose this disorder, they really need to be tested by a psychologist or a psychiatrist who has knowledge and experience with adult AD/HD. Perhaps Jason was depressed, as his doctor had indicated, and

▼

he was merely being swayed by the media to claim this trendy new disorder. It would certainly sound better to Jason to be suffering from AD/HD than to have a serious emotional problem.

2. AD/HD is often associated with other disorders, such as depression, anxiety, passive aggressiveness, and addictions. Sometimes it is hard to determine which is the primary condition or the one that should be treated first.

Jason could very well have AD/HD. And maybe the problems associated with AD/HD have caused him to feel hopeless and depressed. But if his depression has reached a point where it is a serious issue, his doctor might choose to treat the depression first and then address the AD/HD at a later time. Other doctors might disagree and treat the AD/HD first, or treat them both at the same time, but it is a judgment call that each professional has to make on a regular basis.

While AD/HD has specific symptoms, these same symptoms occur in a variety of other emotional problems and disorders. So, when examining a possible AD/HD case, the therapist must not only look for the symptoms of AD/HD, but also rule out several other possible causes of those symptoms. That's why you can't say, "I have AD/HD," after merely checking through a list of symptoms in some book (even this book!). It takes a careful study by a qualified professional.

MIXED REVIEWS

Mental health practitioners in the United States are developing standards for the diagnosis and treatment of adult AD/HD. Some other parts of the world are still debating the existence of adult AD/HD.

We believe that AD/HD symptoms will fall on a continuum from mild to severe. Many people will show mild symptoms, particularly in certain settings. For instance, one might say, "Oh, yes, I am highly distractible when reading my textbooks." Yet that same person might be able to read an interesting novel for longer periods of time.

Others have more moderate symptoms across a variety of settings. These folks are now in an area that we might term "diagnosable." But if they are able to adjust and cope with their symptoms, they may never seek treatment and yet function fairly well in certain jobs.

Still others have obvious symptoms that infringe on their ability to function effectively in a broad range of endeavors. In these severe cases, medication, counseling, coaching, and behavior management are immensely helpful.

One indisputable fact is that the diagnosis of AD/HD is on the rise. Over the past decade, as the airwaves and the printed press picked up the issue, people started lining up at clinics to be diagnosed and treated. Doctors reported huge increases in their AD/HD caseload, and reports indicated that the nation's use of AD/HD-treating stimulants, such as Ritalin and Concerta, also rose dramatically.

Is this good or bad science?

Let's put it this way. People suffered from AD/HD twenty years ago and fifty years ago and even back in 1776. (Some have suggested that William Shakespeare, Isaac Newton, Ben Franklin, and Albert Einstein all had AD/HD. But we don't know how anyone could be certain of this.) What did they do about it back then—before they had books like this one?

They lived with it. Some of them (like Shakespeare and company) may have thrived with it. Others probably found it impossible to get any work done. Maybe some of them went to doctors, and maybe some of them were even treated, but not for AD/HD. Depending on the time period, they'd be treated for depression or dementia or humors or evil spirits. And those treatments wouldn't work, because the real problem—AD/HD—was unknown.

In that historical light, maybe the discovery of AD/HD is a great scientific breakthrough, finally naming this pesky beast that has thwarted human achievement for centuries! The recognition and effective treatment of AD/HD can set children and adults free to live fruitful lives.

Or is it all just hype?

Is the AD/HD craze bad science? Are doctors jumping to diagnose something that doesn't exist?

Maybe some of that was going on in the mid-1990s. Psychologist G. Reed Lyon, Ph.D., a director at the National Institute of Child Health and Human Development, said he was alarmed by both the increased frequency of the diagnosis and the fluctuation of the prevalence of the diagnosis within geographic areas. This would indicate that AD/HD diagnoses followed local trends—like an article appearing in a local newspaper— rather than a natural pattern of occurrence. Lyon suggested that AD/HD was often mistaken for other problems with similar symptoms, such as anxiety, emotional concerns, depression, even a hyperactive thyroid.[2]

But at the same time, Robert Resnick, president of the American Psychological Association, was saying that most clients were being diagnosed properly. Sure, the publicity might have led to some knee-jerk reactions, he allowed, but more likely it resulted in a heightened awareness among educators and mental health workers, so that more people could be properly identified and treated.[3]

The authors of the book *You Mean I'm Not Lazy, Stupid or Crazy?* argued for careful assessment of AD/HD: "We can't emphasize enough that a diagnosis is not a do-it-yourself enterprise. A person with schizophrenia, for example, might have attention deficits, but her treatment would be radically different from that of a person with AD/HD. Using stimulant medication in her treatment would likely have the effect of dramatically worsening her condition. The point is, accurate diagnosis is an essential component of treatment."[4]

We want to add our voices to these cautions. AD/HD is a complex syndrome with very different symptoms and various degrees of severity. It is not something you should diagnose or treat on your own. AD/HD frequently coexists with other diagnosable disorders.

If you have a different condition or an additional condition, such as anxiety or depression, the treatment would be very different. In fact, all emotional disorders affect your activity level, the way you think, and the way you process information. The diagnosis must determine that the symptoms you have are attributable to AD/HD and not to any other condition. This is referred to as "differential diagnosis," and it's the main reason you need to consult with a trained professional.

When I (Tom) was working with the Philadelphia School District, I would frequently get referrals for learning problems and/or attentional difficulties. One teacher had a student she thought was severely disabled.

47

▼

"He can't seem to sit still or pay attention," she exclaimed. "And to make things worse, things he once knew he now doesn't seem to know how to do. What kind of disorder would cause a child to forget how to write his name once he had already mastered the task?" she asked.

As it turned out, it was no disorder. The boy was "merely" experiencing the separation and divorce of his parents. It was a particularly ugly situation that affected the boy's emotions, behavior, and thinking.

No, he did not have AD/HD—and that's the point. He could have been treated for any number of complex mental disorders, but it would have been wrong. He was going through an extremely painful time in his life, and he was being emotionally wounded.

SOMETIMES IT'S NOT AD/HD

You may have a number of the symptoms of Attention Deficit/Hyperactivity Disorder, but that may just be the way you are. In their less exaggerated forms, AD/HD symptoms are merely part of normal human functioning. As one doctor said, "We all have some degree of disorganization, inattentiveness, or impulsiveness. Don't be too quick to assume you have a disorder."

Another reason AD/HD can be difficult to diagnose is that the symptoms are often diverse and may even seem contradictory. There are some symptoms that all people with AD/HD display, such as inattention, but even this is inconsistent. A person with AD/HD can focus on something for a while, and very intently, but an hour later be flitting from one thing to another.

Other symptoms vary widely from patient to patient. Some have hyperactivity and impulse control problems; others can't remember things or always lose things; many others find it hard to follow through on projects or to organize tasks; some can be very organized.

For example, one person might need total quiet in order to study or get work done while another needs background music to work effectively. One person might start several different projects and never finish any of them. Another person may jump immediately from point A on an idea to Z, the final product, without considering the intermediate steps.

HELEN'S STORY

Helen was the first adult I (Michele) diagnosed with AD/HD.

I had been counseling her daughter, Laura, for depression and had discovered that Laura had AD/HD. During the clinical interviews with Helen, as I described her daughter's condition, Helen kept saying, "That sounds just like me." Helen viewed films and read books about her daughter's disorder. She soon began to believe this was her own disorder as well.

Laura's story is inspiring. Once she was treated for AD/HD (with medication and counseling), her grades improved dramatically, her social life improved, and her depression lifted substantially. The change in her schoolwork was so dramatic that school officials called to tell Helen that they were concerned about her daughter—she had to be cheating! There was no other explanation, they felt, for the fact that Laura had gone from Cs and Ds to As and Bs.

Helen began to look at her own life and the difficulties she had always struggled with. Recently divorced, she was hesitantly considering a return to school. This was a fear-some prospect because, like her daughter, she had never done well in school, even though she seemed quite bright. Like Laura, she was accused of not working up to her potential. But now Helen was intrigued by her daughter's success. "Could this also be me?" she wondered.

After I evaluated Helen, it became clear that she was indeed suffering from the same symptoms as her daughter— and had been for her entire life. She had frequently been treated for depression due to her poor self-esteem and underachievement. But those treatments had missed the real problem—AD/HD.

I was able to diagnose Helen's AD/HD, but I could not pre-scribe medication. Unfortunately, her daughter's doctor was a pediatrician and not able to treat an adult like Helen. Eventually, Helen found a psychiatrist who said he would be willing to evaluate and treat an adult with AD/HD even though he had never done so before.

After the psychiatric evaluation with this doctor, Helen returned to me in tears. The psychiatrist had stated that she did not have AD/HD, she was merely depressed. So Helen kept trudging along in psychotherapy, taking medication for depres-sion, which hadn't worked before and wasn't working now. In fact, as she watched her daughter's life dramatically improve, Helen became more depressed and frustrated about her own life.

Almost a year later, we found another psychiatrist who was willing to treat adult AD/HD. This psychiatrist was more familiar with the symptoms of adult AD/HD and the medical management of the disorder. I called Helen and asked if she'd be interested in trying again.

At first she didn't want to do it. She'd had her fill of psy-chiatrists. She didn't want her hopes raised and dashed again. But the image of her daughter's turnaround was strong in her mind. Maybe Helen could try once again to see if she too had AD/HD.

After this psychiatric assessment, the second doctor agreed that she did have AD/HD, and he prescribed medication. Almost immediately, Helen began to notice improvements in her ability to focus and concentrate.

Within a short period of time, Helen was no longer depressed, although she still struggled with emotional issues. She did well in her return to school, making the honor roll for the very first time.

In fact, she was even able to take up a unique extracurricular activity. Helen had become an activist in AD/HD education. Wherever she goes, she talks about AD/HD, urging people to seek proper diagnosis and treatment. She wants to help others avoid the plight both she and her daughter had faced due to unidentified AD/HD and an uninformed physician.

——— Just the Facts ———

▶ Mental health professionals can differ in their assessments and opinions of AD/HD.

▶ The symptoms of AD/HD are diverse and complex and can reflect other disorders.

▶ Beware of self-diagnosis and jumping to conclusions. AD/HD can be accurately diagnosed only by a well-trained professional.

▶ When someone's AD/HD is properly diagnosed and managed, the results in that person's life can be extraordinary.

NOTES

1. David Woods, M.D., "The Diagnosis and Treatment of ADD-Residual Type," *Psychiatric Annals* 16, no. 1 (January 1986): pp. 23-28.
2. Randell Edwards, "Is Hyperactivity Label Applied Too Frequently?" *APA Monitor* (January 1995): pp. 45-46.
3. Edwards, pp. 45-46.
4. Kate Kelly and Peggy Ramundo, *You Mean I'm Not Lazy, Stupid or Crazy?* (New York: Fireside, 1996).

Chapter Four

This is your Brain
on AD/HD

Simply put, AD/HD is a condition of the brain in which the person has disturbances with attention, information processing, and impulse control. For some, the hyperactivity is "internal" only, meaning their brains are active even if their bodies are not. The problem may seem more obvious in those who display behavioral hyperactivity.

Children's hyperactivity often seems to disappear as a child matures, leading some to assume that childhood AD/HD is outgrown. But new research indicates that for most, the symptoms don't disappear; they just evolve with age. Some AD/HD children do outgrow their learning difficulties or learn new coping skills, or they eventually just slow down; but it is now believed that many carry some symptoms (or similar symptoms) throughout adulthood.[1]

> Twenty percent to sixty-five percent of children with AD/HD continue to show signs of the condition into adulthood.[2]

A HISTORY OF THE DISORDER

In the mid-seventies, terms like hyperkinesis and Minimal Brain Damage (MBD) were used to describe children with learning disabilities and attentional problems. These children were usually hyperactive, conduct disordered, and typically displayed severe behavioral and emotional problems.

A kinder, gentler era changed the Minimal Brain Damage to Minimal Brain Dysfunction, but that quickly evolved into the more general term *learning disabled*. This category included all kinds of children's problems. Subcategories of learning disability included math and reading disabilities, developmental delays, auditory and visual processing problems, and of course, attention deficits, some with and some without hyperactivity.

Most of the work and research surrounding AD/HD was done with children, but in the late seventies, adult AD/HD started to be recognized (though at first it was called *Residual* AD/HD).

Professionals now diagnose AD/HD following the guidelines of the *Diagnostic and Statistical Manual of Mental Disorders, Fourth Edition* (DSM IV), which is the bible of diagnosis for psychologists and psychiatrists.[3] The DSM IV describes three primary symptoms of AD/HD: inattention, impulsivity, and hyperactivity.

In order to have AD/HD, a subject needs to exhibit at least six of the symptoms listed for inattention or at least six of the symptoms from the combined list for hyperactivity-impulsivity.

In addition to "six from column A or six from column B," the subject must:

▶ have shown some symptoms before age seven;

SYMPTOMS OF INATTENTION	SYMPTOMS OF HYPERACTIVITY-IMPULSIVITY
• often ignores details; makes careless mistakes	• often fidgets or squirms
• often has trouble sustaining attention in work or play	• often has to get up from seat
• often does not seem to listen when directly addressed	• often runs or climbs when he shouldn't (for adults, feelings of physical restlessness)
• often does not follow through on instructions; fails to finish things	• often has difficulty with quiet leisure activities
• often has difficulty organizing tasks and activities	• often "on the go"; acts as if "driven by a motor"
• often avoids activities that require sustained mental effort	• often talks excessively
• often loses things he needs	**Impulsivity**
• often gets distracted by extraneous noise	• often blurts out answers before questions have been completed
• is often forgetful in daily activities	• often has difficulty waiting his turn
	• often interrupts or intrudes on others

▶ have difficulty from these symptoms in two or more settings (such as work and home);

▶ show "clinically significant impairment" at work or school or with other people;

▶ not suffer from another mental disorder that could explain the symptoms.

▼

Those last two criteria (and especially the last one) prevent self-diagnosis. You can go through the lists yourself and consider your own history and present situation. But only a professional can judge whether your impairment is "clinically significant." And only a trained professional can screen for a variety of other disorders that could be causing your symptoms.

Once a professional has completed an assessment based on these criteria, he or she might diagnose:

AD/HD, Predominantly Inattentive Type;

AD/HD, Predominantly Hyperactive-Impulsive Type; or

AD/HD, Combined Type;

AD/HD, Not Otherwise Specified.

CAUSES OF AD/HD

There have been many theorized causes of AD/HD, including

▶ Prenatal birth trauma

▶ Environmental toxins

▶ Food additives, caffeine, and sugar

▶ An inherited personality style

▶ Parenting style or the home environment

▶ The information, TV, "sound bite" explosion of our society

While these issues may be contributing factors for AD/HD in an individual, most research now concludes that AD/HD is an inherited condition in which the brain does not function normally. Contrary to what logic would dictate, the brain of the person with AD/HD is actually less active than the normal brain. Using a combination of scanning devices and radioactive tracers, scientists measured blood flow to the frontal lobes of the brain. In the brain of a person with AD/HD, this blood flow, indicating brain activity, was lower.[4] Interestingly, in cases where the frontal lobes are damaged (for example, head trauma), the patients often exhibit symptoms similar to AD/HD symptoms, including distractibility, impulsivity, and sometimes hyperactivity. However, in head trauma cases, these symptoms are often much more severe.

While the actual functioning of the brain is much more complex than this brief explanation suggests, researchers are growing more certain about how this all works. They have concluded that there is an insufficient amount of the neurotransmitter dopamine in the brain of the adult with AD/HD. This is a chemical that carries the electrical impulses between nerve cells. Therefore, they reason that the AD/HD brain actually needs more stimulation. And that is why stimulants have been the treatment of choice for years.

When you think about it, it seems strange. Why give a stimulant to a person who's already hyperactive? Don't you want to calm him down? Give him a depressant, for goodness sake!

For years, doctors never really understood why the stimulant worked, but it did work, so they prescribed it. Researchers have now found that these stimulants increase brain activity and blood flow in the brain. But the question remains: Why does decreased brain activity result in hyperactivity and distractibility? Why does the stimulation to the brain reduce these behaviors and curb impulsiveness?

The experts still haven't figured this out totally, but it

seems that the understimulated brain will be driven to seek outside stimulation. It tunes into the radio playing in the next room, it notices the activity outside the window, or it jumps into a new project without considering the consequences. Medicinal stimulants merely provide the needed internal activity to bring the brain into a more normal mode of functioning.

Imagine a classroom of young children (or teenagers, for that matter). Let's say the teacher has a low-energy day. What do the kids do? They're bouncing off the walls! There is no discipline in the classroom, no focus, because the teacher is fighting a cold and feeling blah.

But let's say that teacher takes one of those super-duper cold remedies. The teacher perks up and summons the strength to discipline the class. What happens? Less hyperactivity in the classroom but more productive work.

The brain may work something like that. A person with AD/HD has a weak "teacher" in the brain, and therefore the brain functions like an unruly classroom. The proper stimulation gets that "teacher" functioning again, which focuses the brain on what needs to be done.

Just the Facts

▶ AD/HD has a variety of symptoms, which can be labeled as inattentiveness, hyperactivity, or impulsivity.

▶ While many causes have been suggested for AD/HD, it now appears that there is a physical aspect to the disorder: People with AD/HD have less brain activity, which results in a lack of focus, paradoxically allowing the brain and body to "run wild."

▶ Proper medicinal stimulation can help bring brain function into balance.

NOTES

1. Lynn Weiss, *Attention Deficit Disorder in Adults* (Dallas: Taylor Publishing Co., 1992), p. 21.
2. G. Weiss and L. Hechtman, *Hyperactive Children Grown Up: AD/HD in Children, Adolescents and Adults,* 2d ed. (New York: Guilford Press, 1993).
3. *Diagnostic and Statistical Manual of Mental Disorders, Fourth Edition* (Washington, D.C.: American Psychiatric Association, 2000), pp. 85-93.
4. Zametkin, Nordahl, Gross, King, Semple, Rumsey, Hamburger, and Cohen, "Cerebral Glucose Metabolism in Adults with Hyperactivity of Childhood Onset," *The New England Journal of Medicine,* 30 (1990): pp. 1361-1366.

CHAPTER FIVE

WHO CAN DIAGNOSE AND TREAT AD/HD?

THIS IS NOT A FORMAL TEST FOR AD/HD, BUT IT IS A HELPFUL screening instrument to identify those who might benefit from a formal AD/HD assessment. If you score high, we recommend you contact a mental health professional to have a thorough AD/HD assessment done. Please do not assume you do or do not have AD/HD based on this screening assessment alone.

The Novotni AD/HD Screening Assessment

1. Do you have a lifelong pattern of having difficulty "working up to your potential"?

0	1	2	3
Not at all	Just a little	Yes, I think	Definitely

2. Have you had lifelong difficulty with being able to focus consistently on your work or other activities?

0	1	2	3
Not at all	Just a little	Yes, I think	Definitely

3. Do you have a lifelong history of being easily distracted by thoughts, peripheral sights, or sounds?

0	1	2	3
Not at all	Just a little	Yes, I think	Definitely

4. Have your grades, your interpersonal relationships, and/or your career been affected by these difficulties?

0	1	2	3
Not at all	Just a little	Substantially	Greatly

5. Has it been difficult to keep your self-esteem intact due to these difficulties?

0	1	2	3
Not at all	Just a little	Yes, often	Very much so

6. Do you feel that you struggle in the areas of distractibility and inattention more than most people you know?

0	1	2	3
Not at all	Just a little	More than most	More than anyone I know

7. Do you have a lifelong pattern of having difficulty thinking first before you act or talk?

0	1	2	3
Not at all	Just a little	Yes, I think	Definitely

8. Were you physically active as a child?

0	1	2	3
Not at all	Just a little	A lot of the time	Most of the time

9. Do you frequently feel overwhelmed or frustrated?

0	1	2	3
Not at all	Just a little	A lot of the time	Most of the time

10. Do you have any incidents of head trauma, mental disorders, physical or sexual abuse in your past?

0	1
Yes	No

Now total up your points: _____

If you scored twelve points or more, you would benefit from a formal AD/HD assessment.

If you scored ten or eleven points, there is a chance you have AD/HD or a related difficulty. Consult a mental health professional and ask about the possibility of AD/HD.

If you scored fewer than nine points, there is not a significant indication that you have AD/HD. Still, if you are disturbed by AD/HD symptoms, don't hesitate to be properly assessed by a professional. Once you've been formally assessed, you may find you do have AD/HD or perhaps some other difficulty that can be helped.

WHO CAN HELP?

If you're ready to consult a professional for an AD/HD assessment, how do you sort through the maze of psychiatrists, psychologists, neurologists, and so on? How can you tell who's qualified to tell you about AD/HD?

There are various kinds of professionals in the field. You should be aware of the pluses and minuses of each.

The Psychologist

A psychologist is skilled in the way the mind works. While he or she probably knows a great deal about the physical functioning of the brain, the focus of the psychologist is not medical but mental. How do you feel? How do you think? What makes you do what you do?

A psychologist is able to diagnose adult AD/HD. With training in differential diagnosis, a psychologist can consider and rule out other disorders that may look similar to AD/HD.

A psychologist is also able to provide treatment for adult AD/HD through methods such as counseling, behavior management, and supportive problem solving. While there are different theories and therapies, most psychologists have some training and experience in individual and group counseling skills of a concrete nature (that is, Cognitive Behavioral Therapy, Behavior Management, and Reality Therapy). For those with AD/HD, this type of approach seems to be more helpful than an in-depth psychoanalytical process.

By the time an adult discovers that he or she has AD/HD, there are generally a number of psychological issues that need tending, such as self-esteem, interpersonal relationship skills, lifelong habits acquired to compensate for AD/HD, and grief issues regarding the losses the undiagnosed AD/HD created. A psychologist is well equipped to help with these issues.

If you desire or have been advised to seek medication management, you'll need a referral to a medical doctor or psychiatrist. Psychologists do not prescribe medication, but most psychologists routinely make these referrals and frequently provide help in monitoring the behavioral effects of medication.

The Psychiatrist

A psychiatrist is a doctor of the mind and brain. He or she would also be able to diagnose AD/HD and can treat AD/HD through medication management or therapy (depending on his or her specific training and skills in this area). However, psychiatrists often have a psychodynamic orientation and are not as experienced in the concrete, behavior-oriented, problem-solving, therapeutic process that is often most useful for those with AD/HD.

A psychiatrist can complete the entire process of evaluation, medical treatment, and sometimes therapy. However, a psychiatrist is generally much more expensive than other health care providers.

When a client needs to work on the residual issues created by AD/HD, the psychiatrist may need to make a referral to someone more experienced with counseling.

The Family Physician

What about your family doctor?

A family doctor is usually an M.D. or D.O. with general expertise in treating common ailments. Some family doctors have developed an interest and expertise in diagnosing and treating AD/HD. Just as a family doctor may diagnose and treat someone for depression (which is also in the *Diagnostic and Statistical Manual, Fourth Edition*), some family doctors are diagnosing and treating AD/HD in adults. Family doctors are increasingly willing to provide medical management for clients with AD/HD.

Family doctors are able to diagnose and prescribe medications for disorders within their "area of expertise." It is up to each doctor to decide the parameters of his or her expertise. A family doctor knowledgeable about adult AD/HD has the advantage of knowing you and your medical history well. For most adults, a visit to a family doctor is less intimidating than seeing a psychiatrist. Family physicians may be a good first step for people who suspect attentional difficulties.

The biggest limitation of using family physicians for an AD/HD assessment is their limited training and experience in differential diagnostic issues. Attentional difficulties resulting from other mental health disorders may not be as familiar to them as to a mental health practitioner. Therefore, the family doctor may need to refer you to someone with more expertise if you are not responding to first-level medical interventions.

A referral will be needed for counseling.

The Neurologist

A neurologist is a physician specializing in problems of the nervous system. Neurologists are expensive and often require an extensive neurological workup—EEG testing, etc.—which does not seem to be necessary in the diagnosis or treatment of most cases of AD/HD. This neurological workup, however, can be very important if other neurological conditions, such as a seizure disorder, are suspected or present. A neurologist generally has a more limited knowledge of other psychological causes for AD/HD symptoms and may have difficulty with the differential diagnosis needed for AD/HD.

A referral will be needed for counseling.

The Master Level Therapist or Social Worker

A master level therapist or social worker is trained in counseling, with a master's degree in psychology or counseling. If such counselors have been trained in AD/HD, they are generally able to complete the initial screening stages of an AD/HD assessment. However, you may need to be followed up by a psychologist or psychiatrist to make the differential diagnosis.

Just like the psychologist, a trained master level professional is able to treat the symptoms of adult AD/HD through counseling, behavior management, and problem solving. These professionals generally have training and experience in individual and group counseling skills of a concrete nature.

If it is deemed appropriate, a referral will be needed for medication management.

Professional Comparisons

Psychologist

Advantages
- ► Trained in differential diagnosis
- ► Skilled in concrete individual and group counseling and problem solving
- ► Can help with many AD/HD-related issues

Disadvantages
- ► Need to refer for medication management

Recommendations
- ► Recommended for both assessment and counseling

Psychiatrist

Advantages
- Trained in differential diagnosis
- Able to complete the entire process of assessment and medication management

Disadvantages
- May need to refer for counseling
- May be expensive

Recommendations
- Recommended for assessment, medical management, possible counseling

Family Physician

Advantages
- Familiar with you and your medical history
- Relatively inexpensive
- Ease of getting appointment

Disadvantages
- Limited knowledge of differential diagnosis
- Need to refer for counseling

Recommendations
- Recommended as first step for medical management following evaluation by mental health professional
- Generally not recommended for complex assessment

Neurologist

Advantages
- Skilled in complex neurological disorders
- Able to complete the entire process of assessment and medication management

Disadvantages
▶ Limited knowledge of differential diagnosis
▶ Standard evaluation may include tests that are not necessary for diagnosis of AD/HD
▶ Need to refer for counseling
▶ Expensive

Recommendations
▶ Recommended for difficult cases in which additional neurological conditions are suspected or known

Master Level Therapist or Social Worker
Advantages
▶ Relatively inexpensive
▶ Skilled in individual and group counseling

Disadvantages
▶ Need to refer for medication management
▶ May need to refer or consult concerning diagnosis
▶ Limited knowledge of differential diagnosis

Recommendations
▶ Recommended for counseling for individuals diagnosed with AD/HD
▶ Recommended with reservation for assessment

MAKING THE BEST CHOICE

In addition to being aware of professional qualifications, you need to be aware of specific training, skills, interests, and expertise that a professional has in the area of AD/HD. Since adult AD/HD is still a relatively new field, many professionals have not received formal training about it as part of their schooling. It is up to the individual professional to keep abreast of the subject by attending seminars or workshops and reading professional journals and books in the field. Some professionals are more interested in this area and therefore more experienced than others. Unfortunately, some still fail to recognize AD/HD as a legitimate difficulty and are therefore unlikely to provide the needed help.

If you were to hire someone to clean your house, babysit your kids, or fix your car, it would be reasonable to ask for references so you could check out the qualifications of the person you're hiring. When you're hiring someone to help you with mental health issues, it makes sense to do the same thing. If you think you might have AD/HD, you need to make sure the professional you choose is able to provide the appropriate assessment and treatment. Don't forget to ask about his or her experience in the field.

Unfortunately, many people have such awe of doctors that they find it difficult to ask questions at all, especially if they are questioning the doctor's abilities. Isn't it rude? Won't the doctor be offended?

No. It's your right to know the qualifications of the professional you're considering. They should realize this. However, these professionals are often busy and don't always have time to respond to lengthy questions. So we have prepared a short survey of questions for you to ask.

You don't have to insist on asking the doctor or counselor personally. Usually the office staff can provide you with the information you need to make an informed decision. After each of the following questions we've left space for you to jot down the answers you receive. Feel free to photocopy the page of questions as often as you need to for your personal use.

Five Questions to Ask the Professional

1. How many clients with adult AD/HD have you treated?

2. How long have you been working with adults with AD/HD?

3. What is involved in your assessment and treatment process? (Written tests? Interviews? Family history? Behavior modification? Medication?)

4. What are the costs involved?

5. Have you received any special training in the diagnosis or treatment of adult AD/HD?

One of the most effective methods of finding those familiar with diagnosing and treating adult AD/HD in any given area is to contact your local organization for adults with AD/HD. If you don't know of a local group, contact the following national organizations and ask for information on professionals in your area who might be able to help you.

National AD/HD Organizations for Adults

ADDA
Attention Deficit Disorder Association
1788 Second Street, Suite 200
Highland Park, IL 60035
847-432-ADDA (2332)
www.add.org

CHADD
Children and Adults with Attention-Deficit/
Hyperactivity Disorder
8181 Professional Place, Suite 201
Landover, MD 20785
800-233-4050
www.chadd.org

Just the Facts

Who can diagnose adult AD/HD?
▶ A psychologist, psychiatrist, or neurologist
▶ A master level therapist (recommended for initial screening only)
▶ Please note that the professional must have specific training and expertise in the area of adult AD/HD. Not all professionals in these categories do. See "Five Questions to Ask the Professional" on page 71.
▶ Seek referrals from adult AD/HD support organizations. See the list of national organizations on page 72.

Who can medically manage AD/HD?
▶ A psychiatrist, a neurologist, or sometimes a family physician

Who can provide counseling for those with AD/HD?
▶ A psychologist or master level therapist or social worker
▶ A psychiatrist (depending on his or her ability to provide concrete, structured counseling with a problem-solving versus psychoanalytic approach)
▶ Remember that your problems don't all go away once your AD/HD is discovered and medically treated. There are usually a number of counseling issues that remain.

CHAPTER SIX

THE ASSESSMENT PROCESS

IN OUR HIGH-TECH SOCIETY, WE LOOK FOR HIGH-TECH GADGETRY. So when you're tested for AD/HD, you assume there's a fancy, plug-in, computer-driven, laser-optic, CD-ROM gizmo to magnetically resonate your brainwaves and flash the verdict on a backlit, plasma-flat color screen— right?

Wrong.

Nowadays we generally assume that the more technologically advanced a technique is, the better. But when diagnosing AD/HD, this is not the case. Here's the best technique we have so far:

One person sits in a room telling his or her story to another person.

That's all. No gizmos. Of course, one of those two people should be a professional trained to recognize AD/HD. The other is a person, maybe someone like you, who has a history of inattention or hyperactivity or impulsivity. Oh, there's a structured clinical interview format the professional will use, and there are self-reports to fill out for you and those who know you well. And yes, brain scans can be used to offer more information in some cases.

But there is still no specific medical, biological, or genetic test, computer or otherwise, to diagnose AD/HD.

But this really isn't all that unusual. There are many psychological disorders that have no formal test. Professionals must rely on clinical interviews, observations, and self-report scales to diagnose various problems, such as depression and anxiety. It seems that for some reason, AD/HD has been singled out to generate controversy because it is diagnosed in this manner. This criticism is unfair.

Assessment procedures have recently been developed to aid professionals in the diagnostic process for AD/HD. The Attention Deficit Disorder Association (ADDA) has developed guiding principles for the diagnosis of adult AD/HD.

> One of the most critical steps in properly addressing the significant influence AD/HD has on contemporary society is to establish a standard of care for its diagnosis and treatment. While gaps exist in our knowledge about the precise cause of AD/HD and controversy abounds about aspects of its diagnosis and treatment, research and clinical experience over the past few decades have been sufficient to begin to identify certain principles regarding the evaluation and treatment of AD/HD.[1]

The Guiding Principles for the Diagnosis and Treatment of Attention Deficit Hyperactivity Disorder emphasize the following eight points:

1. Evaluate and treat the whole person.

▼

2. AD/HD should be suspected but not presumed. The professional will need to identify and address potentially coexisting conditions.
3. AD/HD may be present across the life span.
4. A comprehensive assessment is necessary for an accurate diagnosis.
5. The evaluation should be conducted by a qualified professional.
6. Response to medication should not be used as the basis to diagnose AD/HD.
7. Diagnosis should be based primarily upon the DSMIV criteria.
8. Diagnosis should involve others familiar with the person undergoing the evaluation.[2]

The assessment process for AD/HD in adults presents some challenges. According to prominent researchers in the field,[3] these can include the fact that the symptoms of inattention, impulsivity, and hyperactivity are core symptoms of human nature and also common to many other psychiatric disorders; clinically significant impairment is a relative term; it is often difficult with adults to establish a childhood history of AD/HD; and there is no litmus test that pinpoints the existence of AD/HD. Despite the challenges, here's what to expect in the process of diagnosing adult AD/HD.

THE ASSESSMENT INGREDIENTS

The assessment process looks at several pieces when putting together the puzzle of a possible AD/HD diagnosis. These pieces usually include background information, a clinical interview, self-report rating scales, observations of others who know you, a medical examination, and often, formal intelligence and achievement testing. Each piece is important.

Background Information

If you can retrieve your old school records, especially your grades and teacher comments, this may be extremely helpful in the diagnostic process. Many times school records include comments such as "not working up to potential," "unable to focus," "difficulty sitting still." These comments can now be seen as red flags, alerting us to a history of attentional difficulties.

If you have ever been tested for any type of learning or emotional problem, either in school or independently, please try to obtain copies of the reports prior to your evaluation. This information will also help with an accurate diagnosis.

Be prepared to talk about any treatments or strategies you have already tried, as well as their results.

A developmental history will include maternal health during the pregnancy. The known maternal risk factors for AD/HD are: young age of the mother, use of alcohol or marijuana, smoking, toxemia during pregnancy, and extended labor.

Clinical Interview

As you might expect, you will need to meet personally with the professional who is assessing you for AD/HD. The clinical interview will generally take a minimum of four forty-five to fifty-minute sessions (four clinical hours), although it often takes much longer, depending on individual circumstances.

You will be asked about your current difficulties. Are you having trouble at work or home? Is inattention, hyperactivity, or impulsivity becoming a major problem for you?

But the assessment must also include information about your early childhood history: Did you have similar difficulties while growing up? Do you remember times of inattention, hyperactivity, or impulsivity? How did friends and family react to you? Did they think you had a problem in one of these areas? Early childhood information helps in the assessment process. Although AD/HD may change over time, there are generally signs of difficulties in some areas during the early childhood time frame. Unfortunately, some adults have only a vague recollection of their early years and may be unable to obtain input from parents or siblings to fill in the holes. Be prepared to do the best you can. Sometimes, looking over old pictures in a family photo album can stimulate your memory.

The assessment process will include some type of family history section. A genogram (a drawing of your family system) is one useful method to help determine whether or not there might be a family history of AD/HD or other disorders that could impact the diagnosis.

The professional will also ask questions relating to other problems. This is part of the "differential diagnosis," in which he or she tries to rule out alternate explanations for your symptoms. Potential coexisting conditions include: depressive and bipolar disorders, anxiety disorders, chemical and behavioral addictions, oppositional defiant disorder and conduct disorders, learning disorders, psychotic disorders, pervasive developmental disorders, obsessive/compulsive disorders, personality disorders, and tic disorders.

Don't be surprised by questions about the use of self-medicating substances. These can range from stimulants such as coffee, soda, and chocolate to numbing substances such as alcohol or marijuana. Many adults have learned to manage their AD/HD symptoms through these methods.

Professionals may use informal questions to gather all of this information, or they may rely upon a structured list of questions such as the Barkley Structured Clinical Interview[4] or the Diagnostic Form of the Brown ADD Scales for adults.[5]

Self-Report Rating Scales

Most AD/HD assessments include some type of rating scale on which you are asked to rate your current behavior according to several variables. For instance, the Brown Scales have separate questionnaires and separate normative samples for adolescents (ages 12-18) and adults. They are easy to use, score, and interpret. We particularly like these scales because they provide a score that falls on a continuum from Mild to Severe AD/HD, not just "yes, you have it" or "no, you don't."[6]

You may also be asked to complete an inventory or rating scale regarding your behavior as a child. Examples of these are the Wender Utah Rating Scale, the Brown ADD Scales-Adult Version, the Conners Adult Attention Rating Scales, and the Copeland Symptom Checklist.

It should be noted, however, that the self-reports of many adults with AD/HD are unreliable because they often over-report or under-report their symptoms, or they don't remember them. Since most adults have "always been this way," it is often difficult for them to have a clear frame of reference in which to evaluate themselves. To further complicate the issue, many have friends and/or family members who also have AD/HD. So they have a somewhat skewed idea of what is "normal."

In addition to the self-report scales for AD/HD, it is also useful to complete self-report scales such as the Beck Depression Inventory and an anxiety inventory, to check for co-occurring conditions or a possible alternative diagnosis.

Observations of Others

Due to the difficulties with self-observation, it is extremely helpful to have someone familiar with you also attend a phase of the assessment process or be available by phone. This way the professional can get another angle on your situation.

It is also helpful to have parents and/or siblings complete childhood rating scales regarding what they remember of your childhood. They often help provide a comprehensive understanding of your situation, both past and present, across various settings.

I (Michele) had one client who had fifteen of his friends fax me copies of his observation rating scale, all noting very high numbers on many of the AD/HD characteristics. His parents, on the other hand, only reported observing minimal difficulties for him. It turned out that his parents both probably had AD/HD and therefore never noticed the symptoms as being out of the ordinary!

Intelligence and Achievement Testing

In addition to a comprehensive interview and checklist data, many professionals in the field consider some formal testing an important element of the assessment process. Formal testing of intelligence and achievement aids in differential diagnosis (especially with regards to specific learning disabilities), helps assess co-occurring conditions, helps assess strengths and weaknesses, and is very useful in designing strategies for remediation. The assessment of cognitive functions helps to look at "executive functions" and includes activities such as activation, arousal, working memory, recall, planning, and prioritizing.

You may be requested to take an individual intelligence test, such as the Wechsler Adult Intelligence Scale (WAIS-III), or the Wechsler Abbreviated Scale of Intelligence (WASI). Some of the subtest scores can be combined to yield a "Freedom from Distractibility" score that is useful in understanding the impact of attentional difficulties. The purpose of the intelligence test is to evaluate your overall level of intelligence, which will help assess whether you really are having difficulty working up to your potential or whether your expectations are unrealistic.

The Woodcock Johnson Tests of Ability (WJ-III) is the main instrument used to assess achievement. Intelligence and achievement testing are helpful in assessing learning disabilities, which many with AD/HD also have. Although AD/HD creates difficulty with learning, it is not a formal "learning disability." However, some have estimated that between 50 and 80 percent of children and adolescents with AD/HD have a learning disability. Therefore, we can assume that many of the adults who did not "outgrow" AD/HD still have learning disabilities that may also be affecting their ability to work up to their potential. This is important because the treatments for a learning disability and AD/HD are not the same, although they overlap somewhat.

Formal assessment of intelligence and achievement is helpful to understand if and to what degree AD/HD, and possibly specific learning disabilities, have compromised your academic skills. Don't panic if you receive a lower score than you expect on such testing. Please note that your results on such tests may be significantly compromised by AD/HD and/or learning disabilities. Scores are negatively impacted by a lack of attention to detail, hyperactivity, or impulsivity.

Medical Examination

Be sure you have had a complete medical history and physical examination performed within the past twelve months to rule out medical conditions that may look like AD/HD and to identify any associated disorders that may require medical management. Sometimes AD/HD-like symptoms can result from an undiagnosed hearing or visual difficulty. Thyroid disorders, although infrequent, may also mimic AD/HD. This should be checked when there is clinical evidence of hypo- or hyperthyroidism or a family history of thyroid disease.

Although elevated lead levels can produce AD/HD symptoms, this is becoming rarer and can be ruled out through routine blood tests. Certain seizure disorders may also have similar characteristics and can be diagnosed through an EEG if your doctor feels it is warranted.

Other rare (but possible) medical conditions that need

to be ruled out include: Fragile X syndrome, fetal alcohol syndrome, Glucose 6PD deficiency, Autistic spectrum disorders, and phenylkonuria.

A medical evaluation will also help determine whether medication is an appropriate form of treatment for you and which medications would work best. For example, if you have high blood pressure or heart difficulties, there are certain AD/HD medications that you should not take.

"The role of the physician in the evaluation of AD/HD should not be underestimated," says AD/HD expert Russell Barkley, "despite overwhelming evidence that by itself the medical exam is inadequate to serve as the basis for a diagnosis of AD/HD."[7]

Computer Testing

The use of computer testing has grown in recent years. As part of your assessment for AD/HD, you may be asked to interact with a computer to help assess your ability to focus on a task and follow directions. (Aha! Finally a high-tech gizmo!) Examples of computer diagnostic tools are the Test of Variables of Attention (TOVA), the Intermediate Visual and Auditory Continuous Performance Test (IVA), the Continuous Performance Tests (CPT), and the Gordon Diagnostic System (GDS). Each of these tests requires the subject to perform a simple (and probably boring) task for an extended time (usually fifteen to thirty minutes). The computer will measure response times in milliseconds and provide feedback on your ability to attend to task, and impulsivity. In the case of the CPT, there is an infrared motion analysis that can distinguish subjects who are significantly more active than normal.

Although the computer testing may confirm difficulties with attention, it lacks specificity and should not be used in isolation. Especially missed by this type of assessment are the people with AD/HD without hyperactivity or impulsivity. In addition, there is a tendency for the computers to miss the diagnosis with many people who have AD/HD (high false-negative rate). This is because those with AD/HD tend to perform best in a one-to-one task that is novel and of a short duration—exactly the situation created in computer testing. One certainly can't rule out AD/HD based on such a test.

ADAPTIVE BEHAVIORS

Many professionals are also including measures of adaptive behavior as part of the assessment process. These areas can include educational, occupational, relationship, and parenting issues. At the heart of many issues with adults with AD/HD are difficulties working with and living with others. One assessment in this domain for adults is the Novotni Social Skills Checklist as both a self-report and observer form.[8]

UNDERSTANDING THE ASSESSMENT RESULTS

There are three possible results following an AD/HD assessment:
1. You have AD/HD.
2. You do not have AD/HD.
3. It is not certain whether or not the difficulties you are experiencing are due to AD/HD.

If You Have AD/HD

If you have AD/HD, you will begin to understand the ways in which your life has been and continues to be impacted. Possible treatment options that are best suited for the management of your condition will be discussed. We will present this treatment information in the following chapters.

It is also possible that you have AD/HD and some other co-occurring condition. Again, this is common, and treatment strategies for both the AD/HD and the co-occurring condition will need to be discussed.

If You Don't Have AD/HD

If you don't have AD/HD, the professional will recommend further diagnostic testing or other treatments to help with the difficulties you are currently experiencing. Even if it isn't AD/HD, you still have a problem that made you think you might have AD/HD! That problem still needs attention.

One older adolescent was referred for an AD/HD evaluation due to her inability to focus, especially on school homework. As it turned out, she did not have AD/HD but was experiencing emotional difficulties related to interpersonal conflicts. This client participated in individual counseling for a few months and learned to express her feelings rather than stuff them. Her difficulties with concentration disappeared.

If It's Not Certain

Because the assessment process is not an exact science and the issues involved can be very complex, at times there may still be uncertainty at the end of the evaluation. It looks like it could be AD/HD. But then again, maybe it is something else. Despite following a careful assessment process, sometimes you just aren't sure.

If the AD/HD-type symptoms are severe and not readily accounted for by an alternative diagnosis, we recommend treating the person as if he or she has AD/HD. Because treatments for AD/HD are generally quick and therefore easily evaluated, we prefer this approach to working with alternative possibilities first. In summary,

The diagnosis of AD/HD should never be made based exclusively on rating scales, questionnaires, or tests. The evaluation should be designed to answer three basic questions: (1) Are a sufficient number of AD/HD symptoms present and causing impairment, at the present time in the person's life; (2) Have these symptoms been present since childhood; and (3) Is there any alternative explanation for the presence of these AD/HD symptoms?[9]

────── Just the Facts ──────

▶ Guidelines for assessment of adult AD/HD have been developed by the Attention Deficit Disorder Association and are available on their website at *www.add.org*.

▶ There is no specific medical, biological, or genetic test for AD/HD; however, professionals can conduct a thorough assessment. AD/HD assessment standards exist for most professional associations.

▶ The AD/HD assessment should include background information (school records, previous testing results); a clinical interview; self-report scales; reports or interviews from others (family, friends); a medical examination; sometimes formal testing of attention, learning capability, or task performance (computer or IQ); and assessments needed to rule out other co-occurring conditions.

NOTES

1. Attention Deficit Disorder Association, "Guiding Principles for the Diagnosis and Treatment of Attention Deficit Hyperactivity Disorder," *www.add.org* (2001).
2. Attention Deficit Disorder Association.
3. Murphy, Gordon, and Barkley, "Challenges to Diagnosing AD/HD in Adults," *The AD/HD Reports* 8, no. 3 (June 2000).
4. Russell Barkley, Ph.D., *Attention-Deficit Hyperactivity Disorder: A Handbook for Diagnosis and Treatment* (New York: The Guilford Press, 1990).
5. Thomas E. Brown, *Brown ADD Scales: Diagnostic Form* (San Antonio: Psychological Corporation, 1996).

6. *Brown ADD Scales: Diagnostic Form.*
7. Barkley, p. 256.
8. Michele Novotni, *What Does Everybody Else Know That I Don't? Social Skills Help for Adults with AD/HD* (Plantation, Fla.: Specialty Press, 2000), pp. 295-302.
9. Attention Deficit Disorder Association.

PART THREE

RECOGNIZING THE SYMPTOMS

CHAPTER SEVEN

CHANNEL SURFING:
INATTENTION

"I CAN'T EVEN STAY FOCUSED ON MY DAYDREAMS!" ONE AD/HD client said. "I have daydreams within my daydreams! I can be trying to focus on a presentation at work when I start to day-dream. Before I know it, I'm off into another daydream. Sometimes I can have four or five sub-daydreams within my one daydream. All this while I'm trying to pay attention to a presentation at work. It's very frustrating!"

Living with AD/HD is like watching television with a channel surfer. A few seconds of one station, then a few minutes of another, followed by a few seconds of several stations . . .

The major symptom of Attention Deficit/Hyperactivity Disorder is, as you might guess, a lack of attention. This does not mean that people with AD/HD can never pay attention to anything; it means they have a deficit. That is, they cannot pay attention as much, as often, or as con-sistently as others.

Many characteristics of AD/HD vary, such as hyperactiv-ity, which may or may not be present. But nearly every adult with AD/HD has problems with inattention, an inability to concentrate consistently on important tasks or stimuli.

This lack of consistency can be maddening for people with AD/HD. Generally they can get most of the facts in a given situation, but this can be even more frustrating than missing the whole picture. If you know you have no clue about something, you'll ask about it, or you'll avoid situations where you'll need to know these facts. But a person with AD/HD often doesn't know what's missing.

For example, a wife tells her AD/HD husband, "Tonight my last business client is at 4:30. I'll be home after 6:00. I'll bring home pizza for dinner." The husband, however, hears, "Tonight my last client . . . 4:30 . . . I'll bring home pizza for dinner." So when his wife comes home at 6:30 with the pizza, he's upset. He has been waiting for two hours! The wife is frustrated because she's being blamed for something she never said she would do.

Similarly, a student with AD/HD may read the assigned textbook chapter and expect to do well on a test. Imagine her surprise when the questions cover something she has totally missed! Yes, she read the chapter, but her attention drifted away at certain points.

We hear a regular refrain from people with AD/HD who have underachieved in school. They may be quite intelligent, but they cannot study effectively, and so they often fail. Their mental picture of things is something like a slice of Swiss cheese, with holes here and there.

"I can't even stay   daydreams! one ADD
    have daydreams within my   trying to focus
on a presentation at work when I start   Before

I know it, I'm off Sometimes I can have four
or   within my one daydream. All   trying to
pay attention to a presentation at work. It's
very   like watching TV with a channel
surf   one station, followed by a few another,
followed by a few   several stations. . . .
      of Attention Deficit/ Hyperactivity Disorder
      guess, a lack of attention. This does not
mean that people with AD/HD   can never pay
attention   to they have a deficit. That is, pay

When a person with AD/HD reads a page in a book, the information received may "look" like the text above. That's because his or her attention may fade in and out. While this section depicts two-thirds of the information of the previous page, obviously it's nearly impossible to make sense of it.

This is life with AD/HD—getting most or some of the facts, but always needing to fill in the gaps. Some people become quite adept at guessing what they've missed and faking their way through life, but it's a tough game to play, and sometimes they get caught. This can be embarrassing and frustrating.

Sometimes parents, friends, and teachers can misread AD/HD in an intelligent person. One woman we know had a professor who would not believe that she had AD/HD. The professor saw AD/HD as a learning disability or a kind of mental retardation. Because our friend was often very perceptive in class, learning some things quite well, the professor figured she was just making excuses. But AD/HD is not an inability to concentrate, but an *inconsistency* of concentration. These lapses of concentration can create difficulties with memory, organization, interpersonal relationships, and career success.

The inconsistent attention of the person with AD/HD means that one day a household task will get done and the next day it won't; one day an appointment will be remembered and the next day it will be missed. Teachers, employers, and family members who don't understand AD/HD can easily assume that the person with AD/HD is just being obstinate, uncooperative, passive-aggressive, or lazy. "You did this yesterday! Why not today?" Even those who do understand AD/HD can be extremely frustrated with the erratic behavior of a person with AD/HD.

BLINKS

James Reisinger, who has AD/HD himself, has written a booklet in which he refers to lapses in concentration as "blinks."[1] It's a helpful concept.

Everyone blinks. We close our eyes often, for a split second at a time. But what if you blinked and didn't open your eyes for five seconds or twenty seconds or a full minute? What if you opened your eyes after a long blink and didn't know you had missed anything? That would be similar to the everyday experience of a person with AD/HD.

Another friend of ours (without AD/HD) has a habit of falling asleep while watching movies on video. He'll rent a tape and watch it late at night when he's dead tired. He tells us he has "sort of" watched a lot of great movies. This guy is a perfect picture of the "blink" theory. As his eyelids grow heavy, he literally blinks and keeps his eyes closed, drifting into sleep for ten or fifteen minutes. When he opens his eyes, he doesn't realize how much of the movie he's missed. He thinks he's watching the next scene, but he's actually missed five or six major scenes of the movie. Suddenly the characters are talking about things he doesn't know anything about. He has to piece together the plot, but then he drifts off again and misses more. As the closing credits roll, he thinks he has seen 95 percent of a disjointed film, but his wife tells him he was snoring through a third of it.

Similarly, the person with AD/HD generally has no idea how much action he or she has missed. People with AD/HD are always trying to "piece together the plot" of what's happening around them. As one successful businessman explained, "I have developed systems of dealing with things based on incomplete information. I'm not sure when I've had a skip [blink]; I just find out that I have missed things all the time."[2]

Like normal blinking, these distractions are completely involuntary. They just happen. But unlike our friend watching late movies, the person with AD/HD does not drift off into the nothingness of sleep. On the contrary, the AD/HD "blink" is filled with mental activity—"thoughts, images, memories, plans, or calculations that are often totally unrelated to the subject at hand," says Reisinger.[3]

When you have AD/HD, Reisinger adds, your "mind seems to have a dozen open channels to every thought, sound, or sight. Thoughts spring from one to another and then wander on."[4]

For this reason, people with AD/HD tend to be very creative. Their minds are filled with exciting images, bold metaphors, new ways of doing things. Several clients have told us they occasionally stop taking their medication when they need to be creative. They need to let their minds fly free for a while.

Of course the difficulty comes when there's a job to do, a person to see, a meeting to remember, a bill to pay. AD/HD makes it hard to stay focused on the mundane activities of daily life.

Concentration difficulties also escalate with boredom and fatigue. If a person with AD/HD is working on a familiar task, there is an increased tendency to daydream. Or if a person with AD/HD has been focusing on some task for a period of time, he or she may "use up" the supply of concentration and may have difficulty with the next project or task. Concentration is "expensive" for a person with AD/HD.

WHAT WE'RE UP AGAINST

We see several aspects of attention deficit. If you have AD/HD, you might experience any of the following.

Internal distractibility. Thoughts keep popping into your head. You might call this "mental hyperactivity" — the mind is always on the go. If you're listening to a lecture, any word may spin off a series of puns, images, memories, or theories.

External distractibility. Noises get you off track. So will movements you see with your peripheral vision. Yet your power of observation can be quite remarkable.

Once I (Michele) was in a restaurant with my family and I could tell that my son Jarryd, who has AD/HD, was highly distracted. I asked him, "What do you hear?" He proceeded to pro-

vide an amazingly thorough list of all the noises in the restaurant. The people talking in the corner. The dishes clinking in the kitchen. The fork scratching the plate at the next table. The waiter's footsteps. Unable to filter out all these sounds, he naturally found it difficult to focus on the conversation at our table.

Inability to "weigh" data. In writing a book like this, we have a lot of information available, but we have to sort through it. We have to decide what's more important and what's less important. We have to "weigh" the data available to determine which items are worth our (and your) attention. But when you have AD/HD, you have difficulty weighing the merits of different input. In the restaurant Jarryd was hearing a cacophony of sound, but he lacked the ability to sort it. Most people have little problem saying, "That conversation across the room is not as important as the one at this table." But AD/HD makes this a tough task.

Disinhibition. You may have heard the Broadway song "I'm Just a Girl Who Can't Say No." With AD/HD, you have a similar situation. It's what some researchers call disinhibition. At times, you might lose your ability to reject certain thoughts or actions. You receive sensory input and your mind is churning out auxiliary thoughts, and you can't say no to any of it. You follow each sound or thought as it comes, because you're unable to put it in its place.

COMPONENTS OF INATTENTION

The various components of inattention can be defined as difficulty in the following:
▶ Choosing the item to focus on
▶ Ability to keep paying attention

▶ Paying attention to more than one item or thought

▶ Stopping attention to one task to shift to another task

We can see that the lack of "weighing" ability might keep a person with AD/HD from choosing the right stimulus to focus on. Distractibility, external and internal, continually battles with your efforts to sustain the focus over time. The other two components (dividing the focus and shifting focus) have to do with transitions. Even when you succeed at staying focused on one task, the switch to another task can be devastating.

Say a woman with AD/HD is strolling with her husband. He gazes at the horizon and says, "Look at that sunset. Isn't that gorgeous? It reminds me of our first date. Do you remember?"

The wife says, "Remember what?"

The problem is that the husband is asking her to divide her attention. She may have been fine as they strolled, working hard to keep her attention on him as they talked. But then he directed her attention to the sunset, and then to their first date, and she couldn't handle the transition. She could look at the sunset or listen to him, but she couldn't do both.

You may regularly "groove in" to certain tasks, but if you are interrupted, it's hard to get back to what you were doing. A man with AD/HD may be successfully screening out distractions and typing up a report, but if the phone rings and he answers it, he'll forget about the report. AD/HD makes it difficult to shift from one stimulus to another. Transitions of attention are the most vulnerable times for those with AD/HD.

With that in mind, we must say that this is a difficult time to live in, if you have AD/HD. It's a fast-paced age.

MTV revolutionized entertainment by changing visual images every few seconds. Now we see it in the movies, hear it in modern music, and even the billboards change images as we drive by. Distractions abound and transitions are many. In fact, this may be why adult AD/HD has just come to the surface as a widespread disorder. In slower times, people could cope much better. The battle to control their attention was not as fierce. But now anyone who cannot keep up with our go-go culture gets left behind. It becomes more obvious that there's a problem.

"Paying attention"—something most people take for granted—is an ongoing struggle for those with AD/HD. As we have seen, it means you need to:

1. Find the appropriate stimulus and focus on it
2. Sustain focus
3. When appropriate, release this focus so you can move to another stimulus

Each of these steps is difficult when you have AD/HD.

OTHER CAUSES OF INATTENTION

People with a high degree of *anxiety* often find it hard to concentrate. They may be distracted from everyday tasks in much the same way as those with AD/HD. What's the difference?

Primarily, anxiety is a temporary condition. Those who are anxious generally have been able to concentrate in the past. Their current distractibility is a reaction to certain temporary pressures. However, people with AD/HD have a lifelong history of attention deficit.

Anxiety is also limited, in most cases. That is, it tends to occur in only one or two areas of life. A man may be anxious about his job performance, and so he has difficulty remembering details or focusing on a task at work. Perhaps some of that anxiety even carries over to his home life. But put him on a Caribbean beach and the anxiety dissipates along with the distractibility. With AD/HD, you'll still have trouble focusing consistently, even if you are basking on a Caribbean beach.

Depression also creates distractibility and can be as pervasive as AD/HD, affecting all areas of life. But again, AD/HD is distinctly a lifelong disorder. With a thorough case history and differential diagnosis, a professional can determine whether one's lack of consistent attention is caused by AD/HD or depression, or some other problem.

RAMIFICATIONS OF ATTENTION DEFICIT

One study tested people with AD/HD in their ability to attend to and complete a task. It found that their performance goes up and down (refer to graph on page 103). Sometimes they can attend to a task even better than those without AD/HD, but much of the time their attention is far worse.

Because of all that "down time," the researcher concludes, it takes people with AD/HD three to four times longer to complete tasks.

Remember Helen's daughter, Laura, the high school student with AD/HD? Laura tells of times she studied all night for a test and still didn't do as well as her friends who cracked the books for maybe an hour. This is a common complaint of those with AD/HD, who have to work doubly hard (and then some!) to get their work done.

When you consider the cumulative effect or education,

PERCENTAGE WORK COMPLETED[5]

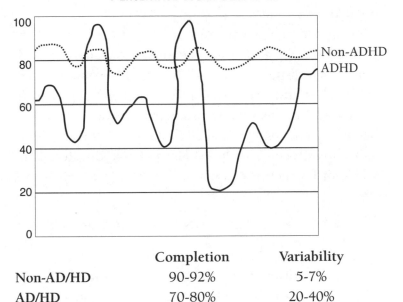

	Completion	Variability
Non-AD/HD	90-92%	5-7%
AD/HD	70-80%	20-40%

the problem becomes even more acute. If a young child was distracted while the class was learning p's and q's, how will he learn to read? He may know 92 percent of the alphabet, but he'll stumble on a lot of words. If a child is "blinking" while the class studies subtraction, how will she ever understand long division?

Because of their increased "down time," AD/HD students are always catching up. They learn to make assumptions, to guess at what they missed, and they can be pretty clever about this. But they still find it hard to master any subject.

The same difficulties can be seen on the job. In business, people often talk about a "learning curve." It takes a new employee a certain amount of time to master a task. But the curve is greatly altered for a person with AD/HD, who can learn aspects of the assignment very quickly but miss key instructions.

So, should people with AD/HD stick to easy, nonchallenging jobs? Not at all! The boredom factor can often yield even greater distractibility. And there's no reason that folks with AD/HD can't be helped to live up to their full potential.

Yet there are also many problems, major and minor, that arise from attention deficit in daily life. Imagine how many hours people with AD/HD lose looking for their keys—or for their tax forms.

Assets of Attentional Fluctuations

As we have said, the same factors that send your mind chasing after distractions can also help you to think creatively. The disinhibition that creates some embarrassing social situations can also create some rather stunning art. Those without AD/HD tend to restrict their thinking to certain "normal," acceptable, predictable patterns. With AD/HD, you can usually break through those patterns.

This wide-eyed perspective is not only good for painters and poets, but also for entrepreneurs. The out-of-the-box thinking that comes with AD/HD can be an asset for high-level executives—if they can find a way to get through the paperwork. Often they have secretaries or friends or spouses who keep them organized while they keep churning out creative ideas.

People with AD/HD can be very observant. Because their senses do not focus tightly on subjects, they are more apt to get the big picture of what's going on. Imagine a couple attending a party. He has AD/HD; she doesn't. As they compare notes afterward, she might report on a few great conversations she had, but he can say what everyone was wearing, who was talking to whom, and how often the punch bowl was filled.

I (Michele) see this "full view of life" in my son, Jarryd. For example, while working on a school assignment at the kitchen table, he will see through the window a red-headed woodpecker, six blue jays, and the beautiful pink sunset. All these things I would have missed, even though I was washing the dishes in the same kitchen at the same time. Because I was focused solely on my task, I would not have seen the sky or the birds.

One of my (Michele's) clients was an inspector of plant operations. He was very good at his job because he saw everything. Nothing escaped his full view of the world. On one visit to my office he said, "You know, the left rear tire on your car looks pretty low. You ought to get that checked." When I took the car to the shop, sure enough, there was a small leak. Only someone with AD/HD would notice a small amount of air missing from a tire of a car over fifty yards away, which he passed on the way to an appointment!

So, in a way, this trait of inattention could really be called *multiple* attention or *fluctuating* attention. While it's inconvenient when you want to focus on one thing, it gives a fascinating view of a world full of wonders.

Recent theories suggest that the gene for AD/HD appeared in ancient civilizations and was passed on because it helped people function better. In primitive cultures, "traits such as novelty-seeking, increased aggression and perseverance" helped hunters hunt, warriors war, and wooers woo, according to one report. "Primitive hunters with this gene would have been more successful and would have been better providers for their families and tribes. These and other factors may explain why the gene is so prevalent now."[6]

Thom Hartmann, a popular AD/HD author and lecturer, has suggested that AD/HD traits were especially appropriate for hunters, but when society changed its emphasis from hunting to farming, those once-valuable traits became a problem.[7] Yet even today, we see people with AD/HD thriving in hunter-like careers—as salespeople, entrepreneurs, and artists.

Six Tips to Improve Attention

1. Battle boredom. Boredom is a deterrent to attention. That's true for people with and without AD/HD. But if you have AD/HD, it is really, really difficult to stay with a boring task.

So do what you can to make tasks less boring. Obviously, this is easier said than done, but you can try to inject humor whenever possible, add drama and suspense to mundane activities, use bright colors, and do tasks in new ways. Try squeezing a ball to help keep your mind and senses stimulated.

2. Reward success. One basic element of behavior management is to offer rewards for the successful completion of tasks. If highly motivated, a person with AD/HD may be able to focus better. That act of focusing is still "expensive"—it uses up a lot of energy—so you may want to reward yourself with a mental "vacation" for a certain amount of time. But be sure to play by the rules. Do not reward yourself when you're "almost" finished; press for the actual completion of the task.

3. **Put up "signposts."** The distracted mind goes wandering over unmapped boulevards. You need to put up "signposts" so you can find your way back to the task at hand. The classic "signpost" is the string tied around a finger to keep you from forgetting something. People put up signs on their mirrors, on their refrigerators, on their car dashboards — "Don't forget this!" Other people make lists of things to do. We keep telling people with AD/HD to *write things down* (especially appointment times with us!).

4. **Simplify your space.** If constant distraction is a problem for you, do not put your desk by a window; face the wall. Do not listen to a news radio station as you work; try a station with monotonous music (such music can help to mask extraneous office noise). Do not put a million things on your walls that might draw your mind away from the task at hand. Keep things simple in your workspace.

This is actually a complex point, because some people with AD/HD need a stimulating environment. They get distracted if an office is too quiet. Know yourself. Know what works for you, and set up your space accordingly.

5. Stop beating yourself up. Emotionally, that is. Many people with AD/HD will attempt a task and then go off on a mental journey of distractions. When they come back to the task, they are full of self-recrimination. "I am so bad. Look at all this time I wasted. I have no self-discipline. I couldn't even do this little thing. Now I'm so far behind." This kind of negative self-talk can actually be a disincentive. You're like the runaway child who finally wants to return home but fears punishment. If your runaway mind expects to receive insults when it finally comes back to the task, it may stay out there a little longer. Change your self-talk. Accept the fact that you are easily distracted. Applaud your own creativity. Jot down new ideas that arise from your mental wanderings. Set reasonable goals for your work, allowing for some "distraction time."

6. Consider medication. For some folks with AD/HD, all the behavior modification methods in the world won't do much good. There are people with AD/HD who have stacks of Day-Timers, who work with bare walls and nonstop Muzak, who promise themselves trips to Tahiti if they'd only get the job done—and still they don't get the job done. When it comes right down to it, AD/HD involves a glitch in the electrical circuitry of the brain. You can't behavior-manage that! But in conjunction with counseling and behavior management, medication can help immensely.

Just the Facts

▶ The hallmark of AD/HD is inconsistent attention, rather than the inability to concentrate at all.

▶ We can think of AD/HD distractions as "blinks," in which a person misses certain pieces of what's going on (but is active in a mental journey of his or her own). This results in a "Swiss-cheese" view of life, full of holes, making it three or four times as hard to keep up in school or work. Many people with AD/HD find success by figuring out or guessing what goes in those gaps.

▶ Inattention consists of an inability to focus on the proper subject, sustain that focus, split that focus between two subjects, or make a transition to a new subject. Those with AD/HD have trouble in all those areas.

▶ With AD/HD, you face external distractions of sight and sound, as well as internal distractions of thoughts that are sparked by words or images. You probably also have difficulty weighing the importance of what you perceive, tending to say yes to every new stimulus (disinhibition), rather than filtering out unimportant material.

▶ There are also many positive characteristics of AD/HD, notably creativity and a "full view of life."

▶ People with AD/HD can use various behavior-modification and psychological techniques to improve their attention, but they should also consider medication.

NOTES

1. James Reisinger, "Blinks: A Phenomenon of Distractibility in Attention Deficit Disorder," P.O. Box 1701, Ann Arbor, MI 48106.
2. Quoted by James Reisinger in "Blinks," *Parents Supporting Parents*, p. 6 (article condensed by Margie Shankin from Reisinger's booklet).
3. Reisinger, p. 5.
4. Reisinger, p. 5.
5. Keith Bauer, *Attention Deficit Hyperactivity Disorder in Children and Adolescents* (Milwaukee: Professional Educational Resources, 1993), p. 5.
6. Bob Seay, *www.Attitudemag.com* (March 2002). Citing an article by Dr. Robert K. Moyzis published in the January 8, 2002 edition of the journal, *Proceedings of the National Academy of Sciences of the United States of America*.
7. Thom Hartmann, *Attention Deficit Disorder: A Different Perspective* (Grass Valley, Calif.: Underwood Books, Inc., 1993; revised 1997).

CHAPTER EIGHT

READY, FIRE, AIM:
IMPULSIVITY

MY (MICHELE'S) CLIENT WAS OUT DRIVING WHEN HE SAW A HOUSE for sale. Now you must understand that he and his wife were not looking for a house. They had not even discussed the idea of moving. But my client had AD/HD, with a large measure of impulsivity. And he liked the house.

So he stopped in to take a look. And he bought it.

It won't surprise you that his wife was angry about that. In fact, that marital tension was the main reason he came to see me.

READY, FIRE, AIM!!!

That's what another client called it—this impulsive quality that affects so many with AD/HD. His mother always said, "Ready, fire, aim," when she complained about the reckless things he did. He almost never thought first before he did something, and that continued to create problems for him as an adult. I'm not referring to an occasional impulsive purchase, such as an unneeded sweater or electronic gadget. I'm referring to clients who may, on a whim, quit a job, buy an expensive car, or decide to move.

One man I (Michele) counseled had switched jobs over 120 times and was in the process of considering another job change. Another client had moved more than twenty times so far, often for no apparent reason.

Steve had an appointment with a colleague and got there ten minutes early. Impulsively, he knocked on the office door and poked his head in, interrupting a meeting in progress.

"I just wanted to let you know I'm here," he said. "The secretary told me to wait, but I just wanted to let you know I'm here."

You can imagine the nods and glares from the people in that meeting. But five minutes later he knocked again and interrupted the session.

"I just wanted to let you know that I have a hard time waiting," he explained.

Steve has AD/HD.

But what's wrong with being spontaneous? Aren't AD/HD people just "living on the edge" a bit more than the rest of us, taking chances, breaking the mold, having fun?

One woman with AD/HD explained the problem to me. Others, she said, may do an occasional impulsive act, but for her it was a lifestyle. For her, control was the exception; impulsivity was the rule. The situations in which she was able to think first and make a rational choice were very few.

"Impulsivity is the second major characteristic of children with attention disorders," says an expert on childhood AD/HD. But get this: "Many consider it to be the most serious and the most enduring problem in adolescence and adulthood."[1]

A fifteen-year study of children with AD/HD found that impulsivity was the most pervasive, troublesome, and longstanding of the AD/HD symptoms.[2]

Hyperactivity in AD/HD children is often outgrown, or at least rechanneled into more acceptable forms of movement. Inattention is a nagging problem for those with AD/HD, but it's largely a private matter, and many people can find ways to cope with it. But impulsiveness gets you into trouble.

What is impulsiveness? Impulsiveness may refer to:

▶ Actions that are executed too quickly or in an unreasoned way

▶ Actions that cannot be withheld during deliberation

▶ Behavior directed in a deliberate fashion toward obtaining immediate gratification at the expense of longer-term goals

▶ Actions that cannot be stopped or altered once they are initiated, even if the consequences of the action might be undesirable or unpleasant[3]

Therefore people appear to be impulsive if they respond before they have thought through their desired response or before they have gained an understanding of the task, and if they are less able to stop or alter their actions once started.

A clinical study by Schachar and Tannock (1993) concluded that AD/HD is associated with a deficit in executive control of action.[4] In other words, the AD/HD mind is like a company without a CEO, or like a classroom without a teacher. Without that controlling force, things can get chaotic.

The study also found that AD/HD is associated with deficits in both response inhibition and response reengagement processes. That is, the mind lacks the ability to say no to an action once it has thought of it. It's like a car without brakes. Once it gets going, it's hard to stop.

Hallmarks of Impulsivity

Difficulty Reaching Long-Term Goals

Many with AD/HD find it difficult to engage in the process of working toward long-term goals. Let's say Gail wants to be a teacher, but four years of college seem like an eternity. So she decides to take a job as a secretary. She's earning income from the start, and there's no need for any long-term planning. However, she may become frustrated. She'll be earning less than she could be earning in a job that required advanced training. She'll be working below her potential, all because she made an impulsive, short-term decision to shuck college for the quick money of an immediate job.

Speak First, Think Later

Impulsivity does not relate just to actions. Adults with AD/HD often have the most difficulty with their tendency to speak first without thinking about the consequences. Obviously, this type of impulsivity can create havoc in interpersonal relationships and careers.

My (Michele's) son, Jarryd, often makes inappropriate statements. He has told me, "I just can't help it. It's like it's connected. An idea comes into my head and it just comes out my mouth. Just one step! There's nowhere to stop it 'cause it's just one step!"

"Just one step." It's that "car without brakes" idea again. You hit the gas pedal and that's it. There's no stopping.

People with AD/HD often feel a sense of urgency. They

must share their ideas before they forget or lose the opportunity. They often will interrupt a conversation or blurt out something that has nothing to do with the topic currently being discussed. Since they also have a difficult time evaluating priorities, it is hard for them to differentiate important from unimportant remarks.

Low Frustration Tolerance

Due to impulsivity, many with AD/HD have a hard time waiting. This often leads to frustration when the world does not give them *what* they want *when* they want it.

In fact, many adults with AD/HD live their lives in a chronic state of frustration. Little annoyances are magnified. A clerk needs a price check and the person with AD/HD seethes with impatience. Why? Does he have somewhere to go? Not necessarily—he just can't stand waiting.

Folks with AD/HD often have a hard time "going with the flow" or being flexible. Experts have suggested that, due to the considerable internal resources needed to compensate for the disorder, people with AD/HD are "used up" and therefore don't have the additional resources needed to deal with these "extra" situations.

Shifting from Task to Task

Another by-product of impulsivity is difficulty completing tasks. Many with AD/HD find it very hard to resist the urge to do something else, especially if they are engaged in a task they're not crazy about.

When Janet* was asked whether any of her family members might have AD/HD, she laughed and said, "I know my mother had it! She even won an award for having the most *unfinished craft projects, and she only showed a portion of them. She always had good intentions but somehow never finished anything. Her life was sidetracked."*

Dan*, another AD/HD client, also had difficulty finishing things. Once I (Michele) was interviewing him with his wife, Carol, who listed the household projects he had started but never completed.

"The worst one," she said, "is the wall he knocked down, intending to put up a new one. That was three weeks ago, and the new wall isn't up yet. It's still just a pile of rubble."

"Oh," I said.

"You don't understand," Carol replied. "It's an outside wall!"

RIGID OR COMPULSIVE
COPING STRATEGIES

Some people with AD/HD may have developed a very rigid sense of structure in order to manage their impulsive behavior. One client, for example, who has become a Marine, finds there the external structure and discipline he lacks internally.

We know one man who is a relentless list-maker. Each day he makes a long list of "things to do," far too long to be completed. There are so many things he wants and needs to do, so he tries to corral them all on paper. Every year he buys at least one schedule book or "personal organizer," but he seldom stays with it through January. Still, his list-making puts some structure in his life. It's one way of coping with his impulsive tendencies.

With some types of AD/HD, the internal filter that processes decisions seems to be impaired. If this is a problem for you, try the following strategies.

Five Tips for Curbing Impulsivity

1. Take time to "aim." Can you relate to the "Ready, Fire, Aim" image? If so take time to "Aim" first by using a slogan, mental image, or visual cue to prompt you to think first. Some have learned to "count to ten" before expressing anger. Try something similar before acting rashly on some new thought.

2. Elicit feedback. Consult with others who do not have AD/HD before making a major decision.

3. Don't keep a lot of money with you. Many folks with AD/HD find it helpful not to carry large sums of cash, a charge card, or a checkbook. That way, if an item in a store tempts them, they can't act on the temptation. By the time they go home for the money, often they no longer have a desire for the item.

4. Tell close friends about your struggle. Confide in close friends and coworkers about your AD/HD. Give them permission to be brutally honest with you if you are doing or saying something out of line. (Then, when they are honest, accept the feedback and make amends.)

5. If you are not getting treatment for AD/HD, seek it. A counselor can help devise coping strategies for your impulsive tendencies, and medication could also help.

Just the Facts

▶ Impulsiveness is a frequent component of AD/HD behavior.

▶ Impulsiveness includes:
  - Acting hastily or recklessly
  - Inability to stop actions once started
  - Difficulty pursuing long-term goals
  - Speaking inappropriately
  - Inability to wait without becoming highly frustrated
  - Shifting from task to task
  - Rigid or compulsive coping strategies

▶ Impulsivity can be effectively curbed with a few simple strategies.

NOTES

1. Edna Copeland and Valerie Love, *Attention, Please!* (Atlanta: SPI Press, 1991), p. 30.

2. G. Weiss and L. T. Hechtman, *Hyperactive Children Grown Up* (New York: Guilford Press, 1986); G. Weiss, L. Hechtman, T. Milroy, T. Perlman, "Psychiatric Status of Hyperactives as Adults: A Controlled Prospective 15-Year Follow-Up of 63 Hyperactive Children," *Journal of American Academy of Child Psychiatry* (1985): pp. 211-220.

3. Russell Schachar and Rosemary Tannock, "Inhibitory Control, Impulsivity, and Attention Deficit Hyperactivity Disorder," *Clinical Psychology Review* 13 (1993): pp. 721-739.

4. Schachar and Tannock.

CHAPTER NINE

DANCING TO A FASTER DRUMMER: HYPERACTIVITY

MARIA IS A BUNDLE OF ENERGY. SHE HAS A WARM SMILE AND A *bubbly personality—and she can't sit still. She never could.*

Growing up with four brothers, Maria learned to climb trees and play football. She was always on the go. Her family figured she was just a tomboy.

She went to a Catholic school and even there she couldn't sit still. The nuns would offer her rewards to sit and pay attention, but her mind and body were always going twice as fast as the rest of the class. Maria found herself withdrawing from her classmates. She just danced to a faster drummer.

In college, Maria set her sights on the medical profession, but she couldn't get through the pre-med courses. She was bright enough, but her mind would go racing elsewhere while she was studying or listening to a lecture. As a result, she knew some aspects of those subjects very well but had huge gaps in her knowledge. Maria had to switch her major to physical education.

Eventually, Maria got work in a hospital's physical therapy center, a job in which her physical hyperactivity could *actually help her. She maintained an interest in fitness, running six miles a day. She married a man who was very patient and supportive. But she was still frustrated.*

"Your self-esteem's always on the floor," Maria says, "because you see everybody rising to the top and you know you could do the same thing and probably better." All her attempts at education and advancement seemed to fail.

Then an article in a magazine caught her eye. It was about Attention Deficit/Hyperactivity Disorder. The symptoms described in the magazine matched Maria perfectly. Maybe there was an answer to her problems.

Maria was shy, however, about claiming this disorder as her own. "At first," she says, "I was afraid people would think I was stupid, an idiot, which I'm not! I was afraid they would reject me, that I would lose friends, that they'd look at me like I was a psycho." Unlike those who eagerly accept an AD/HD diagnosis as an explanation for their mysterious woes, Maria wanted to deny it at first. She was embarrassed by the thought that there might be something "wrong" with her brain.

It took two years of wrestling with the idea before Maria finally did something about it. She saw an article in a local newspaper about an AD/HD seminar sponsored by our counseling office. She put it off. Then she saw a second article and decided to come in to see me (Michele).

With some trepidation, she arrived for the initial interview. "I could hear every single noise in the office," she says. "I could hear the clock ticking. I could hear people whispering. Anything like that."

As she described her experiences, she seemed like a good candidate for AD/HD. She spoke rapidly, darting off to one subject, then another. Despite her nervousness, she was blurting things out with a delightful honesty. I also saw the hyperactivity in her fidgeting hands and tapping feet. In addition, her story of lost potential, disorganization, unbridled emotions, and general frustration was classic AD/HD.

I referred Maria to a psychiatrist who prescribed medication—Ritalin. She returned to me regularly for counseling and joined a group of people with AD/HD for mutual support and sharing.

Shortly after beginning treatment, Maria went back to school for a degree in physical therapy. She found it impossible to take a full course load and still keep her job and tend to her family. But now she has cut down on her course work. "It's frustrating," she says. "A degree that should take two years is taking me three years, but I'll get there."

Maria is choosing to manage her AD/HD by taking her medication only when she absolutely needs it—to study for class or to get through a potentially explosive time at work. "With the Ritalin, it gives you focus," she explains. "It helps you to say, 'All right, today I'm going to do this, this, and this.'

"And through the counseling, I'm learning to prioritize. You see, we people with AD/HD have no concept of priorities, organization, when to call when you're late, when to keep quiet when you're really angry. Counseling helps us learn those things."

Maria's still a bundle of energy. And there are times when her hyperactivity works for her, making her energetic, exciting, inspiring, and fun to be with. But now she knows how to focus when she must.

Adults with hyperactive AD/HD often have a history of hyperactive behavior as children. In most cases, the childhood hyperactivity was much greater than the person's current hyperactive behavior. Why? Either adults gradually learn some control strategies, or they just don't have as much energy as they did before.

WHAT HYPERACTIVITY LOOKS LIKE

Most adults show signs of fidgety behavior rather than the gross (large) motor movements more common of hyperactive children. Although inside they may want to be in constant or at least frequent motion, by the time they have reached adulthood, most adults have managed to contain or suppress the hyperactive component of AD/HD. The remaining signs are usually frequent changes in seat position, frequent crossing and uncrossing of arms or legs, or movements of the foot or fingers, such as tapping. To be less clinical—squirming and squiggling.

Rapid or excessive talking may also be a sign of hyperactivity in adults. "Motor mouth" may be a nickname.

Hyperactivity is frequently misunderstood in adults. While people in general tend to accept hyperactive children, smiling wryly and feeling sorry for the parents, hyperactive adults seldom get the same leeway. Because adults have often learned to manage their hyperactivity to some degree, their occasional outbursts of movement are often judged as willful and inconsiderate.

Fortunately, many adults with AD/HD are able to turn their endless energy into successful businesses. They can be tireless workers in community efforts and volunteer organizations, and often they're great with young people. Many become self-employed to allow themselves the ability to utilize their strengths and hire others to compensate for their weaknesses.

THE CONTINUUM

The physical signs and symptoms of hyperactivity are easiest to see in extremes. One AD/HD client, for example, was constantly pacing around my (Michele's) office during our initial fifty-minute session, and even left the room three times. Many hyperactive adults find it difficult to stay seated for longer than ten minutes without getting up to move around.

But how does hyperactivity differ from merely "high" activity? It's easy to see the difference between a hyperactive adult and, say, a couch potato. But what about the high-powered, Type A executive who rushes from meeting to meeting? Or the person who is merely nervous or dealing with stress? What makes hyperactivity hyper?

There's a continuum here. If we could go to a mall and line up one hundred people in order of hyperactive-fidgety behavior, we would find a wide range.

At one end would be the sloths, trudging from store to store, barely putting one foot in front of the other. (And presumably there's a group of people at home too listless to go to the mall.)

Toward the middle of our lineup would be those with "normal" energy. They have moved at a medium pace through the mall, perhaps visiting five or six stores.

At the high end we have the bumblebees, flitting from one store to the next, picking up this object and that one, going back and forth to check prices, racing through the food court.

Now, how many of these are hyperactive, and how many just have a lot to do? And where do you fit in? Are you more fidgety than ninety of these people in our mall lineup? Ninety-five? Ninety-nine?

But our evaluation goes beyond mere percentiles. The key question is this: Is it interfering with your life? Are there things you cannot do because of hyperactivity? Are there concerts or movies you would like to sit through, but just can't? Are your relationships suffering because you can't engage in lengthy conversations? Is it difficult for you to keep a job because you can't seem to stay at your assigned post?

HYPERACTIVE AD/HD AND
TYPE A BEHAVIOR

Often in response to societal demands, a person may feel stressed and pressured to work quicker and accomplish more. As a result, a hard-driving Type A person without AD/HD can often look very similar to someone with AD/HD. But the hyperactive, impulsive behavior associated with AD/HD is different from the hurried, rushed style of Type A behavior in both origin and intent.

A person described as a Type A personality seems to live life in a continual sense of urgency. Life is a giant pressure cooker. The Type A person has to respond quickly to situations that arise. He or she will often feel anxious, impatient, frustrated.

How does such a person respond to the increasing pressure of new information and rapid change? By speeding up. Robert and Marilyn Kriegel explain it this way: "The harried individual trying to keep up with these changes talks fast, walks fast, and acts as if slowing down to relax is tanta-mount to failure. Life is a continual race against the clock.

"The irony is that, while many Type A's use achievement to justify their behavior, they don't perform nearly as well as they could. They become hyperactive, and rush around trying to do too much, too quickly, and as a result accomplish little of quality."[1]

Some of the same dynamics occur with hyperactive AD/HD. Yet there are key differences that need to be discovered during a complete AD/HD assessment.

In order to have AD/HD, you'd have to have a prior history of impulsive and/or hyperactive acts. Most Type A adults adopt those habits in adulthood in response to job or family pressures.

In order to be AD/HD, these characteristics need to cross all settings. Type A people can often be mellow in family settings or while on vacation, whereas someone with AD/HD cannot turn off his or her hyperactivity.

Five Tips for Curbing Hyperactivity

1. **Physical exercise** is very important in reducing the feelings of uncontrolled hyperactivity. You may need to take several short exercise breaks throughout the day.

2. **Short breaks for rest and relaxation** may help you settle enough to remain on task and in the room you need to remain in. (This is also a good idea for Type A personalities.)

3. **Mental relaxation breaks** can also help, since a hyperactive body is usually accompanied by a hyperactive mind. Take deep breaths and visualize a restful scene. (For some that might be a quiet beach, but others might "expend" some of their surplus energy by envisioning themselves running a marathon.)

4. **The calming techniques of yoga** may also be of benefit.

5. **Medication** is frequently helpful if behavior modification techniques fail. Many clients report the most significant improvement in their hyperactivity is in response to medication management.

Just the facts

▶ Hyperactivity is a major component of many (but not all) cases of AD/HD.

▶ Adults with hyperactive AD/HD almost always report hyperactivity during childhood, though the hyperactivity has usually decreased as they have grown up.

▶ "Squirming and squiggling" is common behavior for people with hyperactive AD/HD. They frequently cannot remain in a room or sit still for very long.

▶ "Type A" behavior may look like AD/HD, but it differs. AD/HD has a childhood history of hyperactivity and it crosses all settings.

▶ Various strategies can be employed to harness one's hyperactivity. Results will be different for different people. Some may need medication.

NOTE

1. Robert Kriegel, Ph.D., and Marilyn Kriegel, Ph.D., *The C Zone: Peak Performance Under Pressure* (New York: Fawcett Columbine, 1984), p. xiv.

PART FOUR

EXPLORING TREATMENT OPTIONS

CHAPTER TEN

MEDICATION

LET ME TELL YOU ABOUT MY SON, JARRYD. I (MICHELE) COULD FILL this book with stories of his adventures, but I'll limit myself to a few highlights. He is a delight, but he's also a handful.

There was the time he jumped through the living room window and landed outside in some bushes. Once he saw some pennies in a reflecting pool at the mall and jumped in to get them. He wore out the staff at six different daycare centers before the age of five. My husband and I found it difficult to take him shopping with us, or to church, or out to eat because of his disruptive behavior. We've been asked to leave stores because of him.

I am a psychologist with an emphasis in behavior modification. Surely I could find a way to modify my own son! We tried various reinforcement and consequence contingencies to no avail. Our methods made absolutely no difference!

Oh, Jarryd was always sorry and regretful. He's not a bad kid. He did not enjoy getting into trouble; he said he just couldn't help it.

On one trip to the pediatrician for a routine evaluation, Jarryd escaped from the office and ran down the hallway at least five times in less than ten minutes, disrupting medical supplies and ripping the paper that covered examination tables. He just would not sit still.

The doctor knew that these behaviors were routine for Jarryd and asked if we had thought of giving him medication. I was a little surprised that a doctor would make such an offhand recommendation without a thorough screening and diagnosis.

A similar thing happened later with a neurologist who was evaluating Jarryd for a possible seizure disorder. Once again, with no more than a quick look, he suggested medication management for AD/HD. All Jarryd had done was run down the hall, crawl under the desk, almost rip the curtains down, and refuse to stay still for an evaluation. But still I was taken aback by the fact that two doctors were so freely peddling their medications.

In retrospect, I think the doctors knew something I did not. Even though I knew that Jarryd had AD/HD from a very early age, I felt that it should be possible to control his misbehavior through behavior and environment management. After all, that was my specialty.

But behavioral methods weren't working. These doctors knew that the medication could help Jarryd's brain to function properly. They could tell, even from brief observation, that he was highly impulsive, hyperactive, and extremely distractible—a very likely candidate for medical intervention. At the time, I felt that they were merely trying to sedate my child, and so I resisted.

Through my entire career, I had been skeptical of medical intervention for inattention difficulties. Given the information available to me at the time, it seemed that the difficulties were not physiological but more due to poor parenting, poor teacher discipline techniques, or lack of motivation on the part of capable students who were not working up to their potential. With proper rewards and penalties, organizational techniques, and a proper understanding of the issues, these students could overcome their difficulties; I was sure of it. Some did. But others failed repeatedly. When they did, I just assumed that someone—teachers, parents, or the students themselves—stopped trying.

But I saw my son trying desperately to "be good" and failing again and again. This was not only threatening everything I believed in professionally—it was breaking my heart.

Then I saw pictures of the human brain from studies on AD/HD conducted by the National Institute of Mental Health. These pictures showed that the brain of a person with AD/HD is physically different from the brain of a person without it. AD/HD is not an emotional disorder or a result of bad learning. There is just some unusual wiring in the brain! The transmitters are not transmitting properly.

It is a physiological problem—and it can possibly be set right with medication to get those transmitters working again.

We tried medication with Jarryd and saw tremendous results. It's not a cure-all. There's still a good bit of behavior management required. But Jarryd is now able to respond to behavioral techniques. Under medication, he is able to control himself. He can be the good kid he wants to be.

This whole experience has led me to a kind of conversion. I did a 180-degree turn and suddenly became an ardent supporter of medication as a piece of the treatment package for AD/HD.

I'm not scrapping my old behavior modification methods, but now I see them as only part of the total package.

When Is Medication Needed?

Only a physician can determine when medication is appropriate treatment for a particular case of AD/HD. In most cases, medication management is recommended as part of a multimodal treatment approach, including education, counseling, behavior management, and group support.

A 1999 study on AD/HD released by the National Institute of Mental Health titled the Multimodal Treatment Study of Children with AD/HD (known as the MTA Study) determined that on average, carefully monitored medication management with monthly follow-up is more effective than intensive behavioral treatment for AD/HD in children. In addition, the combination of medication management and intensive behavioral treatments was also much better than psychosocial treatments alone. This combination also allowed the research participants to be treated over the course of the study with somewhat lower doses of medication.[1] Although this study was conducted on children from ages 7-9, one would expect similar results with adults. In 2002, the field of adult AD/HD advanced as Strattera became the first medication approved for treatment of adult AD/HD. Previously, medications used to treat adults were officially only approved for children and adolescents.

If you have AD/HD, medication will not solve all your problems, but it might give you a solid footing on which to approach your problems. Usually medication will account for a significantly more successful outcome in helping you manage your inattention, impulsivity, or hyperactivity.

Medication is not necessary for all adults with AD/HD. In mild cases of AD/HD, you may do well unmedicated.

At times, just knowing that your symptoms are caused by AD/HD, and not by a lack of intelligence or motivation, is enough to encourage you to develop realistic expectations and creative coping skills. The knowledge itself can break the downward spiral of poor performance and poor self-esteem.

"Now that I know I have an actual disorder," one AD/HD client said, "I can work on rebuilding my self-esteem. I can channel my energies in new ways. I can surround myself with others to pick up and run with my ideas. As long as my problem was invisible, it was impossible to fight back. At least now I know the face of the dragon I am fighting."

WHAT MEDICATIONS ARE AVAILABLE?

For all of the following medications, you must consult a medical professional for possible side effects and to determine which, if any, might be suitable for you.

The medications currently being prescribed for AD/HD generally fall into one of the following classifications:

1. Psycho-stimulants. For example, Ritalin and other methylphenidate products such as Concerta, Dexedrine, and other Dexedrine products such as Adderall and Cylert, which is rarely used.
2. NDRI (Selective Norepinephrine and Dopamine Reuptake Inhibitor). For example, Wellbutrin.
3. Alpha 2 agonists. For example, Clonidine or Tenex.
4. SNRI (Serotonin and Norepinephrine Reuptake Inhibitors). For example, Effexor.
5. SSRI (Selective Serotonin Reuptake Inhibitors). For example, Prozac, Zoloft, Paxil, and Celexa.

6. NRI (Selective Norepinephrine Reuptake Inhibitor). For example, Strattera. Roboxetine is under investigation at this time.

7. Modafinil (Provigil), which is used for narcolepsy, is now being investigated for use for AD/HD alone or in conjunction with psycho-stimulants.

Not all of the molecular mechanisms are fully understood, but it is believed that the anti-AD/HD effects of these various medications are due to changes they produce in the amounts of chemical messengers available between neurons in the brain. These "neurotransmitters" have an impact on brain activity.

Let's look at the most commonly used medications in a little more detail.

Psycho-stimulants

The most commonly prescribed and by far the most effective medication for the treatment of adult AD/HD is the psycho-stimulants. These are the first-line agents and are generally tried whenever it is determined that medical treatment of AD/HD is warranted. Research on brain activity has produced evidence that the attending areas of the brain in children and adults with AD/HD are actually *under*aroused. While it has long been known that stimulants are effective in treating AD/HD, this "paradoxical effect" was hard to explain. Why would you give a stimulant to someone who is hyperactive?

You stimulate the brain to do its work of controlling activity. This is also known as "executive function." Stimulants "wake up" these underaroused areas important to better regulate activity. The typical brain will seek an optimal level of stimulation. When understimulated (assuming you are not asleep), you will seek stimulation. When overstimulated, you will seek less stress. Since the AD/HD brain is understimulated, stimulants merely bring you back to a better level of stimulation. In essence, the medication provides the stimulation, so you don't have to. Instead of jumping from task to task, doing two or three things at once, you can focus on one task at a time—because you don't need that extra stimulation anymore.

Obviously, stimulant medications can be abused when not taken as directed. Physicians might shy away from prescribing a psycho-stimulant due to an individual's history of substance abuse. However, the news media has over-hyped the problem of people with AD/HD abusing these medications, and the actual occurrence of abuse is very low for people with AD/HD since stimulant medication often has a calming effect for them.

It is estimated that approximately 80 percent of people with AD/HD have shown improvement with the use of psycho-stimulants. Common medications in this classification include:

- Ritalin
- Dexedrine
- Concerta
- Cylert
- Adderall

Although stimulant medications are known to make Bipolar Disorder symptoms worse, they can be used after the bipolar symptoms are controlled through other medications. In the past, stimulants were avoided whenever there was any indication of a seizure, tic, or Tourette's Disorder. Physicians are now using stimulants with these disorders when they are controlled along with appropriate medications.

The NDRIs

The Selective Norepinephrine and Dopamine Reuptake Inhibitors are the second line of medication treatment for AD/HD when stimulants are not used. They increase levels of dopamine in the brain, which seems to curb some of the impulsivity and inattention symptoms experienced by those with AD/HD. While these medications are generally reported to be less effective than the stimulants, they have the advantage of being harder to abuse and free of the sexual side effects reported with many of the SSRIs. The most common medication in this category is Wellbutrin.

Medications in this group are excellent antidepressants and they, like all so-called second line agents for AD/HD, may be used along with the psycho-stimulants to treat coexisting conditions such as depression.

Tricyclic Antidepressants

Tricyclic Antidepressants are occasionally used when the physician deems other medications inappropriate. However, their usage has dropped dramatically in recent years, as the side effects seem to be more serious than those of other medications. One of the most serious side effects is heart irregularity. If a doctor wants to use any of these medications, a pre-medication EKG may be suggested.

Common medications in this category include:

▶ Desipramine
▶ Imipramine

▶ Anafranil
▶ Nortriptyline

Alpha 2 Agonists

Clonidine and Tenex have been used by themselves, or in combination with stimulants, to curb some of the symptoms of AD/HD.

Selective Serotonin Reuptake Inhibitors (SSRIs)

These are currently the most commonly used medications for depression, anxiety, and obsessive-compulsive disorders, although used by some to treat symptoms of AD/HD. SSRIs are not the preferred substitute for stimulant medication, but may be used in combination with stimulants when there is coexisting depression, anxiety, or obsessive/compulsive disorder (OCD).

The use of these medications increases the levels of serotonin transmitted in the brain, which some people report to be effective in helping them curb their impulsivity. It also gives them a general sense of well-being. The most common complaints about the SSRIs are headaches and sexual side effects, such as loss of desire or delayed orgasm. Many have reported slight side effects, and some have found that the side effects dissipated within a month or two.

Common medications in this classification include:
▶ Effexor
▶ Prozac
▶ Zoloft
▶ Paxil
▶ Luvox
▶ Celexa

Miscellaneous Drugs

The SNRIs may be used as substitutes for the SSRIs to enhance the Norepinephrine in the relevant parts of the brain of a person with AD/HD. Early reports find them to be somewhat effective with fewer side effects. This category of drug is safer to use with those who have addictive backgrounds and may be safer than the stimulants for patients who have tic disorders.

Provigil and Perceptin both are experimental at this stage.

OBJECTIONS TO MEDICATION

Which Is the Real Me?

"I don't want to change who I am."

"If I get rid of the AD/HD symptoms, will there be anything left of me?"

"Who am I without AD/HD?"

We have heard all of these comments many times over. People are often wary of beginning medication, even for something as serious as AD/HD, because they fear they will lose something of themselves.

For many adults with AD/HD, their identity is closely linked with their disorder. They've spent their lifetime coping with the symptoms—the forgetfulness, the difficulties attending to tasks, impulsivity, and so on. The symptoms of AD/HD have become fused with their perception of who they are. Their sense of self-worth has been dramatically assaulted on a regular basis due to these symptoms—but in some cases they have built a sense of uniqueness upon them. They become "Disorganized Dan" or "Sorry-I'm-Late Sally." They learn to accept these qualities in themselves, and the people around them expect them to act a certain way. Furthermore, they have made lifestyle and career choices based on these AD/HD characteristics.

It is no wonder that some people are hesitant to alter these familiar aspects of themselves through medication management.

Individual counseling is helpful in sorting through these identity issues and evaluating the risks and possible benefits of medication management. If you choose to take medication, counseling is still helpful in dealing with this "identity change."

Who's in Control?

"If I succeed at my job by taking medication, is it really me who's succeeding, or the drugs?" This is another point of resistance to AD/HD medication.

We've told you about Laura, whose school grades changed so abruptly after she began medication that her teacher accused her of cheating. But some people with AD/HD think like that teacher. Somehow, they think it's "cheating" to take medication, because the drug is doing their work for them. They don't take credit for the things they accomplish while medicated. The medication may be doing a great job at work, at school, in the home, or wherever, but the person sees himself or herself as "still the same old failure."

Counseling is generally very helpful in sorting out the issues regarding identity and self-esteem. It's important to understand what the medication actually does and does not do. It's like clearing a logjam: the medication does not make new logs; it just orders the flow so the logs float downstream.

If you have AD/HD and you're taking medication for it, you're still the same person. It's just that your brain is put in better working order. In a way, medication helps you to be yourself; it's the AD/HD that has restricted your self-expression.

If you hire a maid to clean your house, does the house now belong to the maid? No, of course not. It's still your house, and its new, clean condition should enable you to enjoy it more, and perhaps even entertain guests. In the same way, medication sort of "cleans your house," allowing you to enjoy your own thinking and present it to others.

Still, some people feel that they are more in control if they take medication only on an as-needed basis and not all the time. And some types of AD/HD medication can be used in this manner.

I (Michele) had one client, an architect, who found that he was better able to design buildings while not on the medication. Somehow the imagination he needed to dream up new architectural possibilities was diminished by his medication. He decided not to take the medication when he needed to work on creative projects, but to take it when he needed to follow up on details.

If your physician allows, and if you decide to take your medication "as needed," be sure to get input from those around you about *when* it's needed.

We knew one AD/HD client who decided to take medication to get him through his working day, but then to go off the medication while he relaxed at home at night. His wife, however, was not as keen on that arrangement. She felt that there was no point in trying to talk with him and express her views while he was unable to focus and concentrate. On nights when she had important things to talk about, she insisted that he take his medication at home, too.

You might consider it something like wearing glasses. After a long day at work, would you stop wearing your glasses for a while? If you had minimal vision difficulties, you might answer yes. And some with minimal AD/HD may also choose not to take medication during more relaxed, less structured times. If you are severely near-sighted, however, it would be ridiculous to set aside your glasses for any length of time—especially if you had to do anything important. The same is probably true of severe AD/HD.

"Drug holidays," when you go off your medication for periods of time, are no longer routinely recommended. In addition to being aware of the importance of paying attention at work, people are also recognizing the importance of paying attention to interpersonal relationships as well as the ability to manage household tasks.

The key point to remember about medication management is that you are managing your medication; the medication is not managing you. You are giving it permission to help you focus on important tasks. You may choose to take it all the time or only once in a while. But you are choosing. You are in control.

How Can You Tell If It Works?

My (Michele's) father also has AD/HD. At first he was reluctant to try medication, but he eventually changed his mind.

▼

Once he tried the medication, he reported being able to focus for longer periods of time while he worked on his computer. He also took the medication before attending a meeting and noticed that he was able to remember some of what was said.

Over time, however, he became convinced that the medication really didn't do much for him anymore. He would stop taking it for a while. I saw him on several occasions when he was off the medication and I could tell the difference within the first three minutes or so. This amazed my father. As far as he was concerned, the medication had stopped working— it was having no effect. But I could tell almost immediately when he had not taken it.

When he attempted to help fix something at our house when he was on the medication, he would fix the item with minimal fuss. While not on the medication, a simple task would become an all-day project, tools would be broken or misplaced, additional parts would become broken, and directions could not be followed.

At a restaurant, while off medication, he would spill the water, drop food, knock over various items, and go off on tangents during conversations. While on medication, he was able to focus in our bridge group well enough to earn the high score of the night, not spill anything, and follow along with the conversations.

While not on the medication, he could only load, unload, and transfer programs on his computer. While on medication, he was able to create a flyer and develop a mailing list. The difference was very clear to me, though he missed it.

It is sometimes very difficult for those with AD/HD to evaluate the effectiveness of medications objectively. Research indicates that the report of someone close to the client may be more reliable than a self-report. Often, we think, it works like this: The person with AD/HD takes medication for a while and eventually forgets what it was like to be unfocused. Now focusing regularly, he or she fails to see any more day-to-day improvement. Therefore, the person concludes that the medication is less effective and decides to stop taking it. Meanwhile, the spouse and other family members can easily see the effect of the medication.

There is clearly a need for some form of objective as well as subjective monitoring of the effectiveness of medication. Self-reports can also be distorted by a few remaining symptoms that may not be caused by the AD/HD. You might think, "I'm still having problems, therefore the medication isn't working," when the medication is working, and it's isolating those non-AD/HD problems that still need to be dealt with.

We have found it helpful to have both the client and a close observer complete a rating scale on a regular basis to help add objectivity to the medication management process.

It also helps to determine what is not being taken care of by the medication and may need to be addressed through further medical intervention, assessment, or counseling.

In some cases, of course, people are clearly able to notice the differences in their lives in terms of achievement, interpersonal relationships, organization, and dreams. Medication should be monitored closely.

MAKING INFORMED CHOICES

You need to make an informed choice regarding medical management. This requires information gathering — a key component of AD/HD treatment. There are a variety of treatment options, each of which is promoted by different professionals in the field. If you are considering treatment for AD/HD, you need to be able to weigh the pros and cons of the different approaches.

Some doctors and counselors recommend only medication management, while others will only recommend counseling. Among those who recommend medication, some suggest constant use while others say clients should use medication sparingly, only when needed for special events. Some will recommend that you take the least amount possible to get some relief from symptoms, whereas others will recommend that you continue to increase the medication until you reach maximum benefit.

Not all professionals are up-front about their personal biases. This can have a profound impact on your decision-making process.

As with any physical problem, don't be shy about seeking a second opinion. No responsible doctor or counselor would object to that. Also, review the literature available concerning AD/HD. There are several books available that include informative chapters on medication management.[1] Support groups such as ADDA and CHADD (see page 165) are also a good resource for helping you make intelligent treatment choices.

All medications have side effects. These need to be carefully evaluated in order to assess whether the potential benefit is worth the possible risk. Please check with your physician for complete information regarding possible risks for any medication you are considering.

If you have AD/HD, it's important to realize that there

are options and combinations of medications and dose levels that doctors may use in order to treat your unique symptoms. If you do not get positive results from your first trial of medication, don't give up! Take the time to communicate with your doctor and work together to review the problem and discuss other options. Some with AD/HD have needed to try three or four different medications in order to find the one that managed their symptoms most effectively.

Do your homework, consult well-trained professionals, and make informed choices about treatment. You may have a great deal to gain.

──── Just the Facts ────

▶ There are a number of options to consider regarding the medical management of AD/HD.

▶ In severe and moderate cases of AD/HD, medication is recommended as part of a treatment plan that includes education, counseling, behavior modification, coaching, and support groups. Those with mild AD/HD may also benefit from medication. Consult your physician.

▶ Some people resist taking medication because they fear the loss of key aspects of their identity. This underscores the need for counseling along with medication.

▶ Some resist medication because they fear loss of control. Medication can actually improve a person's ability to be in control.

▶ Sometimes people don't know whether their medication is working. But the people around them can usually tell.

▶ A person considering medication for AD/HD needs to make an informed choice rather than a merely emotional one.

▶ Choose the members of your treatment team carefully. All professionals are not equally educated or skilled in treating adults with AD/HD. Don't be afraid to seek a second opinion.

NOTE

1. "The Multimodal Treatment Study of Children with AD/HD."
Archives of General Psychiatry. December 1999.

RESOURCES

Books with information on medication management:

Barkley, Russell A., Ph.D. *Attention-Deficit Hyperactivity Disorder: A Handbook for Diagnosis and Treatment.* 2nd ed. The Guilford Press, 1998.

Copps, Stephen, M.D., and Edna Copeland, Ph.D. *Medications for Attention Disorders (ADHD/ADD) and Related Medical Problems: A Comprehensive Handbook.* Specialty Press, 1996.

Hallowell, Edward M., M.D., and John J. Ratey, M.D. *Driven to Distraction.* Simon & Schuster, 1995.

Kelly, Kate and Peggy Ramundo. *So You Mean I'm Not Lazy, Stupid or Crazy?* New York: Fireside, 1996.

Wasserstein, Jeanette, Lorraine Wolf, and Frank Lefever, editors. *Adult Attention Deficit Disorder.* The New York Academy of Sciences, 2001.

Wender, Paul H., M.D. *AD/HD: Attention-Deficit Hyperactivity Disorder in Children and Adults.* Oxford University Press, 2001.

Wender, Paul H., M.D. *Attention-Deficit Hyperactivity Disorder in Adults.* Oxford University Press, 1998.

Videos on medication management:

Medical Management of Attention Deficit Hyperactivity Disorder: Part 1 Joseph Biederman, M.D., Thomas Spencer, M.D., Timothy Wilens, M.D.

Medical Management of Attention Deficit Hyperactivity Disorder: Part II Joseph Biederman, M.D., Thomas Spencer, M.D., Timothy Wilens, M.D.

Medication for Attention Deficit Disorder: All You Need to Know Thomas Phelan, Ph.D. and Jonathan Bloomberg, M.D.

CHAPTER ELEVEN

COUNSELING

THE TENTACLES OF AD/HD REACH FAR INTO THE LIVES OF those who have these difficulties with attention, impulsivity, and possibly hyperactivity. AD/HD affects your self-esteem, your ability to learn, your career, and your relationships, often wreaking havoc in various forms and to varying degrees. Once AD/HD is diagnosed and treatment is begun, those residual effects of AD/HD still need to be addressed.

Out of necessity, people with AD/HD learn many coping skills. These may be rather ingenious as the person grows up with AD/HD, but once the AD/HD tendencies are being managed through medication or other means, the coping strategies may actually interfere with the person's progress.

For example, many people with AD/HD develop an "uh-huh" habit in conversation. They may have tuned out the speaker, but they don't want to be embarrassed, so they mutter "uh-huh" to indicate that they're listening and that they understand. As a result, they often won't stop to ask for clarification of an obscure point. This is a hard habit to break. People with AD/HD become so good at fake listening that it's hard to listen for real.

Other skills necessary for normal adult life may have been missed during the AD/HD "blinks." These include social skills as well as academic skills. Ordinary perceptions, which most people pick up naturally as they grow, may need to be intentionally learned by the adult with AD/HD who is seeking treatment for the first time.

One client was thrilled the first time he saw his wife get angry. "I always got angry so quick and exploded; I never really noticed her," he explained. "We were having a heated discussion and I noticed her face getting red. I said, 'Hey, you're starting to get angry, aren't you?' It was interesting to watch her. Then she raised her voice and clenched her fist. I watched her in amazement because I had never noticed this before. I commented again on her anger and she got mad and left the room because I wasn't focused on the issue, but I was excited because it was the first time in my life that I had actually seen her get mad before I exploded myself." Now, being treated for AD/HD, he was seeing some social nuances he had missed before, like his wife's display of anger.

This is common. When you're receiving counseling for AD/HD, you might start to see and hear new things—the tones of voice that mean "No" even though the person is saying "Yes" or the subtle cues given when you have overstayed your welcome and it is time to leave. Many counseling sessions are spent interpreting events that have taken place during the week and reframing or clarifying them. In some counseling offices, people with AD/HD even take time to practice new social skills.

AD/HD often leads to a sense of learned helplessness and a poor self-esteem. "There is no sense in trying because I've already tried this a million times before and failed. I'm not going to keep banging my head into a brick wall." Outside encouragement is very helpful in encouraging someone to try again or to try in a different way. Counselors need to work at refining the person's view of self. Some clients are rebuilding a whole new sense of identity.

In addition, there are many family and personal issues that require counseling. Some of these have been caused or made worse by the AD/HD. In other cases, the issues may be independent of AD/HD, but AD/HD has kept the person (or family) from dealing with them. As someone with AD/HD begins treatment, many of these old issues emerge and demand attention. For the first time, the person is able to give them the attention they need.

THE FIVE STAGES IN INDIVIDUAL COUNSELING

We find five distinct stages in the counseling process: The "Aha, I have it!" stage, followed by grief, support, exploration, and dreams.

Stage One: Aha, I Have It!

In the first stage, the counselor needs to help you deal with the feelings the diagnosis has aroused—from despair to joy to everything in between. Some people with AD/HD are elated with the diagnosis; suddenly they have a reason for the difficulties they have faced all their lives. Others become anxious or worried with this new label. Frequently they feel a great deal of confusion, a feeling of being overloaded and overwhelmed with this new information and its ramifications.

Stage Two: Grief

We grieve over losses in our lives, and the newly diagnosed person with AD/HD usually is facing up to some past losses for the first time. Often the person with AD/HD feels regret about missed opportunities, broken relationships, and misunderstandings. "If only I had known about this before, maybe I wouldn't have gotten divorced, maybe I would have been able to finish college, maybe . . ."

Grief is something you go through; you can't take a shortcut. A counselor's job is to aid you in a steady progression through the grief, finally reaching a point of acceptance. "Okay, that's reality. Let's start over."

Stage Three: Support

Often the person with AD/HD feels alone, as if no one fully understands the problems he or she has been facing. There may be exhilaration at the prospect of starting a new journey—picking up skills and knowledge that were missed earlier—but it can also be scary. At this stage, the counselor provides encouragement and advice.

Identity and self-esteem issues can be tackled now in

▼

more depth. You need to develop the confidence that you can be a consistently valuable, productive member of society.

As you deal with your AD/HD, you might need help to fully realize your strengths, gifts, and talents. People with AD/HD generally have the ability to think "outside the box," to think of things in new ways, pulling in ideas from a variety of sources. In an age of specialization, this is a valuable commodity. People with AD/HD tend to be very real, open, and honest, not superficial. They are often able to "see through" phony people and empathize with others who are struggling with various issues. These are all good qualities that a person with AD/HD can enjoy and, in a sense, be proud of.

Support groups or therapy groups can be extremely helpful at this stage in the process.

Stage Four: Exploration
In some ways, you might say that a person with AD/HD in treatment is learning how to live. He or she is exchanging old coping skills for healthier new habits, acquiring new life skills, and gaining information that might have been missed the first time around.

This is an exciting stage of counseling. Old problems are addressed and new alternatives are explored. It doesn't have to be the same old story over and over again. You can try things a different way now that you have an explanation for your behavior.

Stage Five: Dreams
What would you like to do now? If the exploration stage was exciting, the fifth stage is positively inspiring. At this

point you can move forward on your own, propelled by dreams of a satisfying future.

One woman in an AD/HD support group was fifty-two years old and had hit a "glass ceiling" in her job. She was never considered for an administrative position due to her inability to organize material. But once she was diagnosed with AD/HD and began treatment, a world of opportunities opened to her. By the time the support group stopped meeting, she was considering taking a new job as a company's national director!

It's never too late to start dreaming. What are your dreams?

Group Therapy

At a certain time in the counseling process, a therapist may suggest that a client join a therapy group. It can be highly therapeutic to share your problems and progress with others who are in the same boat.

We should make a technical distinction between an AD/HD therapy group and an AD/HD support group. An AD/HD support group is often organized and led by persons with AD/HD who usually don't have a professional counseling background. Generally, the purpose is to share information rather than to work on individual issues. An AD/HD therapy group is organized and led by a professional counselor with experience in AD/HD and in group therapy. The purpose of the therapy group is to provide information and to work on the individual AD/HD-related issues each member is struggling with as well as emotional issues and concerns.

Therapy groups are generally time-limited — ours are six to ten sessions. The groups meet for one-and-a-half hours each week. We spend half of each group session in a structured educational talk and the other half in open discussion.

Therapy groups are a powerful tool for healing the wounds of AD/HD. It's often an individual, silent struggle when you have this disorder. It is immensely encouraging to know there are others like you. You are not alone.

What to Expect in Group Therapy

At the first meeting of an AD/HD therapy group, everyone seems apprehensive. "Who will be there? What will they look like? I know that I'm not the only one who has made such a mess of my life, but will these other people understand me or judge me?"

It's usually a diverse group. We're always taken aback by the different forms and faces of AD/HD. In one group we had three with hyperactivity and three without hyperactivity. It was hard to believe they all suffered from the same disorder until they began to share their stories. The common thread became clear as the stories unfolded.

In our groups, we make a point of generating a list of positive characteristics of AD/HD. We are well aware of AD/HD's difficulties, but few people have thought much about its positive components. This process always becomes a highlight of the group process as members begin to see positive characteristics in themselves.

We also have lively discussions regarding treatment options for managing AD/HD. Almost every group has some discussion regarding the use of medication. Another common topic: alternative strategies for managing AD/HD.

"The group was a most valuable piece of putting my life back together," said one of our group members.

"It was good to hear other people talk about how it is for them," said another, "because it was reassuring to know I'm not the only one. I'm not losing my mind."

Yet another said, "I have gained a much better understanding of myself and how AD/HD has affected my life. The group has also helped to build my self-confidence and determination in dealing with and overcoming my negative AD/HD ways. It has been great to be able to relate to such a wonderful group of people."

If you can find an AD/HD therapy group in your area, we urge you to give it a try.

Just the Facts

► Counseling is a necessary component of AD/HD treatment because of:
  - Previous coping skills that now hinder growth
  - Missed social and academic skills that need to be learned
  - Learned helplessness and low self-esteem
  - Other personal and family issues that arise after an AD/HD diagnosis
► The AD/HD counseling process consists of five stages:
  1. Aha, I have it!
  2. Grief
  3. Support
  4. Exploration
  5. Dreams
► Group therapy is extremely helpful as adults with AD/HD compare notes, share ideas, and offer support.

CHAPTER TWELVE

BEHAVIOR MODIFICATION

WHAT SHOULD YOU DO IF YOU DON'T WANT TO TAKE MEDICATION? Or if the medical alternatives seem too drastic to you? There are behavioral treatment options for you that will not change your brain chemistry or the way you think, but can help to alleviate some of the most negative characteristics of the disorder.

Mark needed help adjusting his schedule and organizing his life. He worked as a salesman in an office, mostly doing phone solicitations. He was very good with people and did well on the phone. He could build relationships with new clients and turn them into steady customers. But as you might guess, paperwork was his downfall. He would usually fall well behind in turning in his sales reports, and his financial figures were often wrong. The more he struggled, the more he avoided dealing with it, and the further behind he became.

Things got so bad that Mark sought help in order to save his job. Through counseling, Mark reordered his life. He set up a weekly routine in which every Wednesday and Friday he stayed off the phones completely. On those days, he shut his office door, had all his calls held, and focused on writing up the orders from the previous day or two. He used a calculator for his figures and checked his work twice. His clients learned to reach him on Monday, Tuesday, or Thursday, and Mark learned to stay current on all his work. He also spent Friday afternoon cleaning off his desk and organizing his files.

The result was not increased sales, yet Mark was able to maintain his income level while feeling much better about himself and his job. Life became manageable! Mark learned that he needed to keep a routine that forced him to stay organized and focused.

Most people with AD/HD need some sort of lifestyle or behavioral change in order to better manage their lives—even if they are on medication. The MTA Study[1] cosponsored by the National Institute of Mental Health and the U.S. Department of Education found the combination of medication management and behavioral treatment to be the most effective treatment for children with AD/HD. When used independently, they found medication management superior to behavioral therapy. Although not studied directly, it makes sense that this combination would also work for adults with AD/HD. There are several simple tools that can make life much more productive and fulfilling.

BEHAVIORAL TECHNIQUES

AD/HD affects different people in different ways. As you seek behavioral ways to cope with AD/HD, you first need to figure out which behaviors you want to cope with.

During your assessment for AD/HD, you fill out a "problem checklist" of some type. That will give you a place to start. Or you can use the following checklist to isolate the areas of your life most affected by AD/HD.

We recommend you work through these behavioral issues with a professional counselor to ensure one-on-one observation, accountability, and feedback. However, the "problem checklist" may give you a running start on some of the issues you're dealing with.

Problem Checklist

Check all that apply to you.
- ☐ 1. I need to learn more about AD/HD.
- ☐ 2. I do things impulsively.
- ☐ 3. I am always on the go; I need to slow down.
- ☐ 4. I need help learning to better handle my emotions and frustrations.
- ☐ 5. I need to build my self-image.
- ☐ 6. I find it hard to control my temper.
- ☐ 7. I need to overcome a substance abuse issue.
- ☐ 8. I need help in organizing or scheduling my life.
- ☐ 9. I have a hard time putting my tasks in order and doing the most important things first.
- ☐ 10. I need help organizing and handling my finances.
- ☐ 11. I start things but don't finish them.
- ☐ 12. I need help planning my day and following through on that plan.

☐ 13. I forget things too often.
☐ 14. As a student, I am having difficulty keeping up with my classes.
☐ 15. I don't communicate well with others.
☐ 16. I want to be a better listener.
☐ 17. My closest relationships are in trouble.
☐ 18. I need a quiet place to work.
☐ 19. At work, I have difficulty focusing on one thing at a time.
☐ 20. I don't think I've found the right job for me yet.

Go back over the things you have checked and choose three that stand out as your worst problem areas. Circle these.

Then get a different colored pen or pencil and go through the list again with a spouse, family member, or close friend. What does that person see as your greatest challenges? Circle the top two or three mentioned by this person.

Now, from the issues circled, choose the three you want to work on the most. List them here along with the problem number.

1.

2.

3.

Look at the following section for your particular problem areas to see how you might begin to address them.

Problem 1: Education

Information is a powerful tool in coping with AD/HD. It can minimize frustration, build self-confidence, and help a person choose wise strategies for living.

You have already started the education process by reading this book. You can build on this by contacting both of the national support groups—ADDA and CHADD—for more information.

The primary organization for adults with AD/HD is ADDA, the Attention Deficit Disorder Association. ADDA is dedicated to helping adults with AD/HD live better lives. They provide hope, empowerment, and connections worldwide by bringing together science and the human experience. You can contact ADDA by phone at 847-432-2332 or visit their website at *www.add.org.*

CHADD stands for Children and Adults with Attention Deficit/Hyperactivity Disorder. CHADD started out by focusing on kids and educating their parents about AD/HD. But as adult AD/HD became more prevalent, CHADD expanded its outreach to include adults as well. CHADD's resources include books, tapes, videos, and a list of support groups available around the country. Call 800-233-4050 to reach their national headquarters, or visit their website at *www.chadd.org.*

ADDitude magazine splits its emphasis between children and adult issues. It comes out six times a year and maintains an active website at *www.additudemag.com.* The phone number is 888-762-8475.

There is also an A.D.D. Ware House catalog that lists available books, tapes, and videos. Call 800-233-9273 to receive this free catalog of products, or visit their website at *www.addwarehouse.com.*

Because AD/HD research is constantly being done and scientists are always learning more about the disorder, be alert to breaking stories in the media about new discoveries. Every year or so you might scan a library's database (or the Internet) for new articles on AD/HD. Or the AD/HD Report is a wealth of information on the latest research (800-365-7006).

Problem 2: Impulsivity

Impulsivity is a major symptom of AD/HD. It may manifest itself in relatively minor ways or in potentially devastating ways.

Review chapter 8 on impulsivity, especially the suggestions on page 117.

Problem 3: Hyperactivity

Hyperactivity is another major symptom of AD/HD. It is seen mostly in children, but many adults also display hyperactive behavior, even though it may be somewhat muted. Hyperactivity can be physical or verbal.

Review chapter 9 on hyperactivity, especially the suggestions on pages 125-126.

Problems 4–7: Counseling Issues

Many issues of identity and emotions are raised by AD/HD. This is why counseling is an essential part of the treatment process—not only to learn new ways to act but also to learn new ways to think and feel about yourself, about others, and about AD/HD.

Review chapter 11 on counseling.

▼

Problems 8–12: Organization

High school and college students sometimes take extra courses in study skills to help them manage their schoolwork. Adults with AD/HD usually need something similar—some training in "life skills"—to help them manage their lives.

See chapter 15 on organization, especially the suggestions on The Three Ss summarized at the end of the chapter.

Problems 13–14: Learning

Learning problems affect adults with AD/HD as well as children, although they are most obvious in organized classroom situations. College students with AD/HD often have trouble keeping up with course work because of attentional inconsistency. Once they fall behind, it's hard to catch up. Many people with AD/HD keep fighting this battle as they enroll in adult education courses to make up for what they missed in college.

But even those who don't take classes can experience "learning disability" in trying to learn new material for work, church, or home. Additional information can be obtained through the LDA (Learning Disability Association), 4156 Library Road, Pittsburgh, PA 15234; *www.ldonline.com.*

See chapter 16 on learning, taking special note of the suggestions on pages 228-229.

Problems 15–17: Relationships

For many with AD/HD, the most painful part is the havoc it plays in their relationships. Marriages have broken up due to AD/HD. Some people with AD/HD have been alienated from their parents or siblings or closest friends.

Communication is crucial to any relationship, and people with AD/HD need to pay special attention to this (which isn't easy!). Helpful resources include *What Does Everybody Else Know That I Don't? Social Skills Help for Adults with AD/HD*[2] and *A.D.D. and Romance*.[3]

We deal with communication and other issues in chapter 17 on relationships. Take special note of the suggestions on pages 245-248.

Problems 18–20: Work

AD/HD often makes it difficult to find the right job. A helpful resource is *Finding a Career That Works for You*.[4] It may also be difficult to do all the necessary parts of a job, or to get along with coworkers. Often there are problems with the workplace—it's too noisy or too distracting.

If this is a problem area for you, be sure to read chapter 18 on work-related issues, taking special note of the suggestions on pages 264-267.

— Just the Facts —

▶ For several reasons, some people with AD/HD prefer to use behavioral treatment options alone, instead of medication. Even in cases where medication is used, however, behavioral changes are essential for the proper treatment of AD/HD.

▶ Adults with AD/HD tend to have unique challenges in the following areas:
- Education
- Impulsivity
- Hyperactivity
- Identity and emotions
- Organization
- Learning
- Relationships
- Work

▶ This chapter points you in the right direction for addressing each of these problem areas.

NOTES

1. The MTA Cooperative Group. Mediators and moderators of treatment response for children with attention deficit-hyperactivity disorder. The Multimodal Treatment Study of Children with Attention Deficit Hyperactivity Disorder. Arch. Gen. Psychiatry, 1999. 56:1088-1096.
2. Michele Novotni, *What Does Everybody Else Know That I Don't? Social Skills Help for Adults with AD/HD* (Plantation, Fla.: Specialty Press, 2001).

3. Jonathan Halverstadt, *A.D.D. and Romance* (Dallas: Taylor Publishing Company, 1998).

4. Wilma Fellman, *Finding a Career That Works for You* (Plantation, Fla.: Specialty Press, 2000).

▼

CHAPTER THIRTEEN

COACHING

KOBE BRYANT HAS ONE. SO DO VENUS AND SERENA WILLIAMS. Virtually every Olympic athlete has at least one. We're talking about coaches. Maybe you could use one, too.

Why do the greatest sports stars in the world use coaches? Aren't they good enough without extra instruction? Why do business leaders hire consultants? It's not that they're incapable of succeeding on their own, but it helps to have some extra help. We all can benefit from an extra pair of eyes to help us see our blind spots. Sometimes we need a pat on the back or a kick in the butt. We benefit from the help of experts in deciding where to go and how to get there. Coaches are a good idea—in sports, in business, and in life.

This is especially true when you have AD/HD. Coaches can fill in the gaps of your attention. They can remind you of the big picture when you're focused on the immediate moment. They can help you see the details if you get stuck on the big picture. And when you're discouraged, they can provide encouragement.

Where can you find a coach? There are professionals who can fill this role for you. Perhaps your therapist can suggest someone. We'll also include information on some coaching organizations. On a more casual level, you might already have people coaching you in various ways. Spouses, parents, and friends often find themselves pressed into service. We don't want to underestimate the value of these helpers, but we do urge you to consider hiring a professional coach who is trained to assist with the unique challenges of AD/HD.

When I (Michele) was writing *What Does Everybody Else Know That I Don't?*[1], a book on social skills for those with AD/HD, I wanted to include a chapter on coaching. So I turned to one of the pioneers in the field, Susan Sussman, who wrote that chapter for me. Most of the ideas in this chapter come from Susan, and we're grateful to her.

How can coaches help you? Susan says we should think of their work as four Ss: Support, Skills, Structure, and Strategies.

SUPPORT

Sometimes at a health club you'll see someone working out with a personal trainer. It looks almost comical at first. One person is straining to lift weights, grimacing, and popping veins. Sweat is pouring out. Every ounce of energy is channeled into the push against the barbell. And what is the trainer doing?

Cheering.

"Come on! You can do it! Just two more. Good, just one more. Great, now why not try one more? Just one. How about another? Come on. Don't let this weight beat you. You're a winner. Just do it!"

One talks while the other sweats. And guess which one is getting paid.

But that personal trainer is *coaching*. The first job of any coach is support. We all work harder and better when we know someone's on our side. Life can be a struggle, with people scolding, misunderstanding, and demanding way too much. We all need cheerleaders to boost our spirits.

A coach's support can take many different forms, as we saw with that personal trainer. "You can do it!" turns quickly into "Don't let this weight beat you!" if that's what's necessary. Generally, a supportive coach is positive, but sometimes a coach has to offer a challenge.

Encouragement is the most important form of support, especially when you have AD/HD. It's easy to get down on yourself when you forget something important or when people misunderstand you. A coach can bolster your attitude, giving you a clear picture of your value as a person.

But, believe it or not, *nagging* is another form of support—when it's done right. If you have a spouse or parent or friend who keeps reminding you about things you forget, it can get annoying. But a good coach knows how to nag without tearing you down. A supportive nag is *not* saying, "You're so dumb! How could you forget this again?" Instead the feeling is, "I care about you, so I want to make sure you remember all the important things you need to remember." The tone of voice and the underlying attitude are crucial.

Another seemingly negative form of support is the *challenge*. A good coach will challenge you to be the best you can be. That means not letting you get away with shoddy performance.

A friend of ours is a high school play director. Teenagers generally need a lot of encouragement, and our friend provides that. But every so often he has to yell at the students:

"This play stinks! How can you do stuff this bad?" The students are shocked. How could such harsh criticism come from their nice, encouraging director? Doesn't he care about their feelings?

Yes, but he also cares about their lives. If he helps them feel good about a second-rate effort, is he really helping them? If they never learn to push themselves to be their best, they'll be missing out. The criticism and encouragement both flow from the same fountain of support. Because he believes in their ability, he knows they can do better. And he says so. (Notice that the critical comment is directed at their performance rather than at them as persons.)

Coaches can also provide *practical support.* Just as a personal trainer might step in and pick up a barbell from a struggling lifter, so a coach can ease your burden in tough times. Say you're tempted to make an impulsive (and foolish) business decision—a coach can talk you down to earth. A coach can't make up for every bad decision, but there's usually a wealth of good advice that a coach can offer.

Connections are yet another type of support. You may have been burned in relationships and then turned away from people. A coach will help you connect with organizations that focus on AD/HD, with books that offer insight on AD/HD, with a qualified counselor if you need one, and possibly with other people who understand the challenges of AD/HD to help you restore connections in your life.

SKILLS

Ron* once tried to learn Hebrew. He was late to enroll in the class, so by the time he joined, they were already in the second semester. To make up for that, he had picked up the text-

book and had studied the first semester's material on his own.

So far, so good. On the first day of Hebrew 2, Ron took a seat in the classroom, eagerly awaiting instruction. The professor went to the board and started writing in symbols Ron didn't understand. He was stunned. Had he been studying the wrong language?

Well, no. But the prof was using a cursive script, unlike the printed form of the letters that Ron had been studying. As with English, the difference between printed letters and cursive script can be substantial.

It took three weeks for Ron to feel comfortable with the cursive letters. By then he was hopelessly behind. He had missed out on some basic skills in this language, and he never overcame that.

Maybe you can relate. People with AD/HD often feel the way Ron did in that Hebrew class. You've learned a lot on your own, but you've missed some important skills along the way. You may feel that you're always playing catch-up.

A coach can help by teaching you some of those basic skills. What skills are we talking about?

We might call some of them *life management skills.* These include things like: paying your bills the day you get them so you don't misplace them, or at least choosing a place to put the bills you receive; throwing away junk mail after you look at it; writing your appointments on a calendar; using a watch with an alarm; and communicating your activities with your family.

Life isn't easy. Daily we're bombarded with information and responsibilities. It's hard to keep track of it all. Many people develop skills to organize their lives, or at least habits that keep their lives tidy. When you have AD/HD, you process information differently. Sometimes you can juggle eighteen assignments in one day, but sometimes you can't. As a result, many folks with AD/HD never learn organizational skills, because they don't always need them. A coach can help you gain those skills for when you do need them.

Work skills are sometimes the same as life management skills, but they're tied specifically to your occupation. If you're in sales, you'll need one set of skills; if you're an artist, you'll need another. A coach will take time to get to know what you do and what skills you need to thrive in the workplace.

Social skills are another set of behaviors that many people take for granted. But they're not "granted"—they're learned. And if you have AD/HD growing up, your blinks and blanks might have kept you from picking up some very basic stuff. When the other kids were learning to say Please and Thank-you, you might have been pondering the theory of relativity.

I (Michele) have noticed this with my son Jarryd, who has AD/HD. He's a nice kid, but he doesn't always act with "common courtesy." It's not only Please and Thank-you, but things like looking at people while listening to them, talking for a short time and then letting the other person respond, saying good-bye before leaving the room. He's not trying to be rude, but sometimes people think he is. Apparently these things had just slipped through the gaps in Jarryd's attention.

One of the problems with social skills is that everyone assumes that people just know them automatically. If you don't know them, there's no remedial class to sign up for.

You're just "different." People might even shun you because your behavior's a bit odd. So once again, people with AD/HD can have trouble fitting in, and they don't know why.

A coach can help immensely with social skills. You're not unteachable—you just need someone who cares enough to tell you what you're missing and someone smart enough to figure out what those social skills are. "If you're listening to someone talk, look at the person and nod if you're interested. But don't stare. You really only need to look at the person about half the time he or she is talking." That's the sort of thing a coach will tell you.

Jim *has always had trouble starting and maintaining social relationships. He's thirty now, living by himself in an apartment, and working in a family-owned business. With the cooperation of his therapist, he came to Susan Sussman for coaching.*

The problem was clear: he wasn't maintaining eye contact. No matter how long he engaged in conversation with people, he couldn't look them in the eye. Was this some deep-seated fear of rejection that kept Jim from opening up? Well, if it was, that was the therapist's business. Susan's job was to coach him, helping him to gain this skill. She held practice conversations with Jim, encouraging him to increase his eye contact.

She also gave him an interesting assignment: make videos of family members interacting. Together, he and the coach analyzed these tapes, picking up information about appropriate eye contact in different situations. Over several months, Jim's eye contact improved—and so did his interpersonal relationships.

STRUCTURE

The third major area of a coach's assistance is structure. You can develop skills you need to deal with day-to-day challenges, but you still need to structure your life to go where you want to go. You need to get the big picture, not just everyday snapshots.

Matt was a young man with AD/HD who had a loyal group of friends. They all joined together in a fantasy baseball league. This is where you choose a roster of major league ballplayers and total up their stats week after week. It was great fun for Matt and his buddies, and they always had something to talk about.

The problem was, Matt's team wasn't very good. He was always tinkering with his roster. Whenever he got a good player, he would impulsively trade him away. Based on day-to-day statistics, he would trade for players who had temporary hot streaks, but when they cooled off, his team was worse than when he started.

Then a couple of those friends took him aside and tried to show him the big picture. "Here's how you can build your team. Get these good players when they're just starting out and hang onto them! Forget the daily stats and think in terms of the full season." Matt was smart enough to see the logic; he just needed some encouragement to counteract his craving for immediate success.

We won't bore you with the tactics of fantasy baseball management, but the result was that Matt's team got better. The following year—as he stayed with his long-term approach—he made the league playoffs. Maybe next year he'll win it all.

▼

Those friends were doing what coaches do, providing a structure that Matt could use to improve his situation.

A couple of key words have arisen in business circles lately: *reactive* and *proactive*. If your business is always reacting to the latest crisis, you might survive, but you won't get far. Strong businesses are proactive, which means they make the first move. They know where they're going and how to get there. Those business leaders can tell you what they want their company to look like in five years, in ten years, and beyond.

You need to be proactive in your life, too. Sure, it's tough when every day brings a hundred new challenges. It's hard to think about swimming the English Channel when you're struggling to stay afloat. That's why you might need a coach's help in getting that big picture. Where do you see yourself five or ten years from now? What can you be doing *now* to help you get there?

STRATEGIES

Jennifer had a fifteen-page paper to do for a college class, and she was obsessing about it. "I can't possibly write that much!" she complained to her boyfriend. "How can I ever do fifteen pages?"

"One page at a time," the boyfriend answered.

He wasn't just being a smart aleck. That was actually a helpful strategy. He began asking Jennifer about the topic, eventually breaking it down into five different parts. Then he chose one of the parts. "Could you write three pages about this?" he asked.

"I'm not sure," Jennifer replied.

So they talked some more, breaking down that part of the

▼

subject into three sub-parts. "Can you write one page about this? And about this? And about this?"

"I think I can," she answered, and so the fifteen-page paper got written—one page at a time.

Coaches often do what that boyfriend did. They take a huge task and break it up into smaller ones. They help you find a strategy for tackling a project that seems impossible.

When you have AD/HD, often you can become over-whelmed with all the things you have to do. Every moment brings something new to deal with. With all these items clamoring for your attention, it's hard to decide which is most important. A coach can help you set priorities.

Structure and strategies are related. Structure is the big picture; strategies give you a daily plan. A coach might help you gain structure in your life by asking what you want to be doing five years down the road. That structuring might even involve major mileposts along that road—getting a degree, getting an entry-level job in that field, getting pro-moted. But then strategies add flesh to those bones. Going for a degree? Great. Where? When? How will you pay for it? When do you need to start getting catalogs? When should you start filling out applications? Those are the strategies.

A coach can also give you ways to manage your AD/HD symptoms. If you're hyperactive, a coach can suggest methods of channeling your energy—for instance, taking a walk during your coffee break. If you're impulsive, a coach can teach you ways to delay your responses so you can think about them.

Dan* was a bright young lawyer, but also a hothead. On several occasions, his angry outbursts almost got him fired. His coworkers felt as if they were constantly walking on eggshells around him—never knowing when he might explode.

Recognizing that this had been a pattern throughout his life and that it was getting worse, Dan sought coaching. Maybe a coach could help him break that destructive pattern.

The coach asked about Dan's background and learned that Dan had been taking medication to treat his AD/HD for years. But he didn't take it on a regular basis. He also didn't have a good way to report to his prescribing physician the benefits and/or side effects of the medication. Together Dan and his coach developed a medication log—a report of exactly when he took his medication, and when some of his problem behaviors (temper tantrums or interrupting other people's conversations) occurred. He could then go to his physician with this log, showing exactly how the meds were affecting his actions—or weren't.

Besides this monitoring, Dan also developed strategies to manage his anger. Like many with AD/HD, Dan sometimes felt flooded by emotional sensations he had no control over. But at least he could learn strategies to prepare for those sensations and deal with them. People with epilepsy, diabetes, or migraines can often anticipate episodes because of a certain aura they feel and can therefore take measures to protect themselves. In the same way, those with AD/HD can also learn to read the signs of an impending tantrum and then take precautions.

Now, with some practice, Dan can sometimes feel the onset of a volatile episode. These signals remind him that these are times for thought rather than action.

AD/HD can seem like a huge roadblock on your journey toward success and happiness. A good coach will help you find ways through it.

How It Works

As we said earlier, many of the coaching functions can be performed by the people closest to you—your family, friends, and coworkers. But if you want expert help—proven strategies and experienced know-how—look into hiring a professional AD/HD coach. Costs vary, but generally coaching is less expensive than psychotherapy.

Coaching takes place by phone or e-mail, and occasionally through face-to-face meetings. Be sure to check the background of a coach before you sign up. Is he or she experienced with AD/HD? Does he or she have good references? (Don't be shy about asking.) Sometimes a counselor can help you connect with a good coach. For your convenience, we list some coaching organizations below. But you still need to check out your individual coach to make sure it is the right match for you.

One crucial ingredient to a good coaching experience is *your* commitment. If what you are doing isn't working, perhaps it's time to make a change. Are you willing to make changes in your ways of doing things?

Coaching Organizations

ADD BRAIN WORKS
Director: Nancy Ratey, Ed.M., MCC
264 Grove Street
Wellesley, MA 02181
Phone: 617-237-3508
www.addbrain.com

American Coaching Association
Director: Susan Sussman, M.Ed., MCC
P.O. Box 353
Lafayette Hill, PA 19444
Phone: 610-825-4505
www.americoach.com

Catalytic Coaching
Director: Sandy Maynard
1722 19th Street NW #508
Washington, DC 20009
Phone: 888-REFRAME
www.sandymaynard.com

Limitbusters Coaching Academy
Director: Eric Kohner, CPPC
1840 N. Berendo Street, Apt. 102
Los Angeles, CA 90027
Phone: 213-953-8494
www.limithusters.com

Optimal Functioning Institute
Founder/CEO: Madelyn Griffith-Haynie
Phone: 518-482-3458
www.addcoach.com

Just the Facts

► You could benefit from individual coaching to help with specific behavioral issues.
► Coaches can help in four main areas:
  • Support
  • Skills
  • Structure
  • Strategies
A list of coaching organizations is provided.

NOTE

1. Michele Novotni, *What Does Everybody Else Know That I Don't? Social Skills Help for Adults with AD/HD* (Plantation, Fla.: Specialty Press, 2001).

CHAPTER FOURTEEN

ALTERNATIVE TREATMENTS

THE WORLD HAS LEARNED A LOT ABOUT AD/HD IN THE PAST decade or two, but there's still a lot we don't know. We know more about its effects than its causes. And we have found certain ways to manage AD/HD through medication and behavior adjustment, but if you're looking for a cure—sorry, you're out of luck!

People keep looking for a sure-fire remedy, some miracle pill that will make the problems go away. We shouldn't knock it. That desire keeps the pressure on scientists to find more and more effective ways of treating AD/HD. But in the meantime, it can stir some controversy.

Alternative treatments for AD/HD have been suggested—from various diet restrictions to vitamin additives, from biofeedback to acupuncture. But do they work? Are there dangers? Should you look into these treatments?

The answer is a resounding *maybe*.

We're going to briefly examine the most popular alternative treatments and then discuss the best strategy for you. Please do not jump at any of these treatments before you know what's involved—physically, emotionally, and financially. For the most part, these methods have not been proven to the generally accepted scientific standards. However, studies as well as anecdotal accounts of success offer support for each. Bottom line: there are *no* guarantees, and there might be some dangers. Proceed with caution.

DIET

In 1974, a California doctor published a book called *Why Your Child Is Hyperactive*. His answer? Because food contains too many chemical additives. The Feingold Program caught on, and many parents began carefully screening their children's diets for artificial additives. While it's certainly a good idea to make sure a child eats right, scientific experiments showed that normal food additives had no effect on children's behavior. Feingold supporters protest that these experiments failed to control for all additives and that solid research that supports this and other nutritionally based treatments has been overlooked.[1]

Next came the sugar craze. Parents banned sugar from their children's diets, and many claimed it improved behavior—but again, science found no connection between sugar and AD/HD.

More recently, food allergies have been blamed for AD/HD. Maybe hyperactivity and attention problems are just responses to certain foods, some would suggest. This can be tested with a "few-foods diet," which starts with the basics and then adds individual foods until a problem arises.

While some families have found connections between a child's behavior and certain foods, there is no strong scientific evidence yet of such a link—and there is no evidence that this occurs in adults other than for those with a specific food allergy.

NUTRITIONAL SUPPLEMENTS

Maybe it's not that you're consuming too much of something; maybe you're not getting enough. That's the logic of another set of treatments. Actually, the evidence of early experiments is favorable. Perhaps certain supplements can help.

"Antioxidants, flax seed oil, fish oil, evening primrose oil, pine bark extract (pycogenol), grape seed extract, [and] co-enzyme Q10 are among the many products now touted to calm behavior and boost attention," explains one magazine overview.[2] But don't rush out to the drugstore to stock up just yet. Evidence is still being gathered on these substances, and some might be harmful if you take too much.

Scientists have theorized that AD/HD may be related to low levels of amino acids, at least in children. And yet amino acid supplements might have some risk. Treatment with various substances related to amino acids (tryptophan, tyrosine, and phenylalanine) has shown short-term results—two or three months. Writing in the *Annals of the New York Academy of Science*, L. Eugene Arnold notes that "amino acid supplementation . . . may have a role in temporary relief while arranging or initiating other interventions."[3]

Ongoing research on fatty acids is promising. These substances form an essential part of the membranes of the neurons that fire up our brains and nervous systems. Children with AD/HD have been found to be deficient in some fatty acids. In one study, young adults treated with a fatty acid (DHA) showed less aggression.[4]

And so flax seed oil, fish oil, primrose oil, or other sources of essential fatty acids (or the substance *l*-carnitine, which assists fatty acids) might be helpful supplements for those with AD/HD. *Might* be. Stay tuned for further research.

What about your basic vitamins and minerals? Research has shown that a simple multivitamin supplement can be helpful, as some with AD/HD are deficient in certain vitamins and minerals. Megadoses of multivitamins seem ineffective. Megadoses of *individual* vitamins might have an effect, but the treatment is not well tested yet. The same goes for mineral supplements such as iron, magnesium, zinc, or calcium. They might help, but we just don't know yet.

BIOFEEDBACK

With EEG biofeedback, you get hooked up to a machine that shows your brain waves in action. As the theory goes, your brain works in certain rhythms. Those with AD/HD are thought to have different rhythms than others. If you can learn to control the images you see on the feedback screen, you can learn to control some brain rhythms and thus have more control over your brain activity. Some people have used EEG biofeedback with good results, but the scientific studies are just beginning.[5, 6]

A different kind of biofeedback (EMG) has been used along with relaxation techniques and sometimes hypnosis to calm those with hyperactivity. Experts differ on the value of EMG biofeedback. It seems to be less effective than conventional AD/HD treatments, but it might be helpful for those who have trouble taking medication to control hyperactivity.

MEDICAL POSSIBILITIES

Scientists have begun to study a range of medical issues related to AD/HD. It's possible that AD/HD is affected not by a food allergy but by a germ that your body has trouble fighting. Thus immune therapy might be helpful. Perhaps a fungus is the culprit and antifungal therapy is in order. For a while it seemed that the thyroid gland was the hidden problem of most people with AD/HD, but now it appears that only a few people are affected. Still, if tests show poor thyroid function, thyroid therapy could help. Research on animals has also shown that lead poisoning can result in hyperactivity, and so your doctor might want to check your blood for lead levels. If this is a problem, it can be reversed through a process called chelation.

Note that the issues might be different for different people. No one is saying, "Aha! All AD/HD stems from, say, fungus!" (Well, if they are saying that, they're irresponsible.) There are various possibilities that might affect you, and you should ask your doctor about them.

OTHER POSSIBILITIES

Traditional mixtures of Chinese *herbs* have done well in tests with children who have AD/HD. St. John's wort (hypericum) has been used in Europe to treat AD/HD and is believed by some to help with depression, which often accompanies AD/HD.

Acupuncture has not been studied enough as a treatment for AD/HD.

Meditation training seems to have some benefit for AD/HD, but more research is needed.

Massage has proven helpful in preliminary tests, especially the massaging of neck, shoulders/upper back, and along the backbone. And it makes you feel good.

In *mirror treatment,* a mirror is placed in front of a person as he or she does certain tasks. Theoretically, it helps with self-focus, which is sorely needed by many with AD/HD.

Some say that *inner-ear problems* affect AD/HD, and so they've tried medicine for motion sickness. However, there is not much evidence to support this treatment.

Sensory integration is a rather new treatment with computers and machines that offer visual or aural stimulation that must be responded to. Theoretically, there's some validity in the idea that those with AD/HD have difficulty integrating the input their brains receive, but these methods are still being developed.

EVALUATING ALTERNATIVE TREATMENTS

So far the best-proven remedies for your AD/HD symptoms are the ones we've outlined in *previous* chapters, namely medication and behavior modification. Counseling and coaching will also help you deal with emotional and practical issues. You might be impatient with your medication and attempts to change your behavior, but they're still the best methods we know. You might be tempted to try some super vitamin or a hot new herb, but no one really knows whether these will work.

We do know that medication and behavior modification usually have a positive effect.

Still, having said that, we don't want to slam the door on promising new methods. Maybe there's something out there that will help you. But be careful.

PROBLEMS WITH ALTERNATIVE TREATMENTS

1. *Ignoring proven treatments.* The biggest problem with some alternative treatments is that you'll forego helpful treatments or discontinue your medication or behavior modification in hopes that this new method will cure you. We know that medication and working on those organizational habits and social skills are effective. If you're trying some new treatment, add it to the program, but don't drop everything else.

2. *Harmful side effects.* With some of these treatments, the potential downside is worse than the upside. Don't take megadoses of multivitamins. There's little value and possible harm. The herb *kava*, for instance, has been linked to liver damage. Amino acid supplements should also be treated with care. Any major addition to or subtraction from your diet should be carefully monitored and checked by a doctor.

3. *Getting your hopes dashed.* AD/HD is enough of a roller coaster already. Watch out for treatments that make unrealistic claims. They will only disappoint you and possibly kick you into depression. From the start, assume that any alternative treatment has a moderate-to-low chance of working for you. And even if it proves effective, it won't solve all your problems.

With that realistic perspective, you'll better prepare yourself emotionally. (Note also that some treatments seem to work for a time, but then stop working.)

4. *Getting cheated.* "I've been around long enough to recognize snake oil when I see it," wrote one doctor in an Internet chat room. He was referring to alternative treatments for AD/HD. We're not saying that all alternative treatments are being sold by hucksters out to make a quick buck, but be wise about what you spend. Biofeedback and other computer methods can be quite expensive. Some might try to sell you huge supplies of vitamins or herbs. Of course you would spend exorbitant amounts on a cure, and that would be worth the expense, but these methods are still unproven to the scientific community standards. Don't mortgage your house on a risky enterprise.

Anecdotes, Placebos, and Prejudice

When someone tells a firsthand story of how he or she successfully treated AD/HD, you're going to listen. That anecdote means a lot. After all, here's a real live person with a true-life story, and if it worked for him, whatever the treatment was, why couldn't it work for you?

Anecdotes are so convincing that we sometimes accept them from secondhand or thirdhand sources. "I have a cousin who works with a guy who used to grind up shoe leather and smoke it, and it totally cured his hyperactivity."

Scientists scoff at anecdotes, and here's why.

It's just one case. They're used to experiments with hundreds or thousands of subjects.

▼

It's not a controlled experiment. What other factors were involved? And maybe it was the shoe *polish* and not the shoe leather.

Can you believe it? Especially when it's second- or thirdhand, you have to suspect that the story has been embellished along the way. Even firsthand, people like to over-report their successes.

Various causes. Maybe the kid next door got treated for lead poisoning and it cured his AD/HD. Does that mean your AD/HD is lead-related? Maybe, maybe not. But don't rush to get the lead out—get your blood tested first. There are many cases of AD/HD that have nothing to do with lead; maybe yours is one of those.

What works for someone else might not work for you. How old was the person in the anecdote? What gender? What size? What was his or her medical history? There are many factors, just within your own body, that might affect the situation. You can't assume that a 98-pound, 98-year-old woman will have the same results as a 200-pound teenage boy. This is especially important with AD/HD, because there's been so much attention given to it as a childhood issue. You might hear stories of how the kid down the block "cured" her AD/HD, but that might not relate to your case as an adult.

The placebo effect is another factor to watch out for. If scientists are testing a new drug, they'll give the pills to some people, but then they'll have another group (a "control group") that gets fake pills. These fake pills are called placebos. Why do they bother giving the control group pills at all? Because they want to make everything equal except for the actual substance in the pill. When people take a pill, they expect to get better, and sometimes just that expectation makes them better. In fact, studies have shown that the placebo effect can be as high as 33 percent. That is, a third of the people get better without any active medication—just because they expect to.

So let's say you read an ad for *ADDendum*, the hot new herbal supplement that will make your AD/HD a distant memory. (We are just making this up, folks.) You send away for it and get a huge bottle of pills (for only $199.99). And you start taking five pills a day, as directed on the label.

How will you feel the next day? More in control? More able to focus? Less hyperactive? Less impulsive? Maybe. There could be nothing but baking soda in those pills, but you'd still feel better because of the placebo effect. You expect to feel better. What's more, you *want* to feel better. Even more, you *have* to feel better, or else you'll know you're a complete idiot for shelling out two hundred clams for some worthless pills!

Time will tell. The placebo effect will fade. You might try some treatment method and imagine some success in the early going. But wait to see if it lasts.

STAY TUNED

Of course, you're not an expert in medicine or psychology. You rely on the wisdom of others. If you have a doctor or counselor you trust, by all means, follow that person's guidance. But there are many other voices in the treatment world, many of whom have hidden prejudices. We're not saying they're right or wrong, but you ought to be aware of them.

Some have a scientific mind-set that rejects any alternative approach. If a particular treatment hasn't had twenty double-blind, placebo-controlled verifying experiments over a thirty-year period with thousands of subjects, they feel it's highly suspect. Chemicals are good; herbs are questionable; meditation is kind of silly.

Others have an opposite bias. There's a back-to-nature movement that emphasizes the healing properties of all herbs and tries to avoid chemicals of all types. In addition, anything "spiritual"—involving life force or centering—is worth a try.

We are exaggerating the issues here, of course. Most people are somewhere between those two extremes. As you seek advice, you should be aware of the possible bias of those who are advising you.

As for us, we lean toward the scientific side, but try to stay open to new methods that seem to work. Since the study of alternative treatments in the AD/HD field is fairly new, we all have to rely on anecdotal evidence more than we'd like to. But remember, all treatments once started out this way! There just isn't the hard experimental evidence that we'd like. So don't totally discount the anecdotes of people you trust—just don't jump in with both feet yet.

The field of AD/HD research is growing rapidly. There is much still to be learned. As we saw with so many of those treatments we listed earlier in this chapter, the jury is still out. Adequate testing has not been done. Even those that seem promising—fatty acids, herbs, massage—don't have enough data yet.

So stay tuned for further developments. If you're computer savvy, do occasional Internet searches on the subject.

Ask your doctor or counselor from time to time about the latest research, attend conferences, and keep your ear to the ground for fast-breaking news.

NOTES

1. Michael Jacobson and David Schardt, *Diet, AD/HD & Behavior: A Quarter-Century Review* (Washington, D.C.: Center for Science in the Public Interest, 1999).
2. Jamie Talan, "Unconventional Medicine," *ADDitude* 2, no. 6 (June 2002): p. 61.
3. L. Eugene Arnold, "Alternative Treatments for Adults with Attention-Deficit Hyperactivity Disorder (AD/HD)," *Annals of the New York Academy of Science*, p. 316.
4. Arnold, p. 316.
5. Andrew Abarbanel, "Gates, States, Rhythms, and Resonances: The Scientific Basis of Neurofeedback Training," *Journal of Neurotherapy* 1, 2 (fall 1995): pp. 15-38.
6. Thomas Rossiter and Theodore LaVaque, "A Comparison of EEG Biofeedback and Psychostimulants in Treating Attention Deficit Hyperactivity Disorders," *Journal of Neurotherapy* (summer 1995): pp. 48-59.

PART FIVE

OVERCOMING AD/HD
DIFFICULTIES

CHAPTER FIFTEEN

ORGANIZATION

JANE'S HOUSE WAS SO DISORGANIZED THAT SHE HAD STUFF LITERALLY stacked thigh-high in several rooms. Walking through her bedroom was like parting the Red Sea—there was only a narrow path in which to walk and a small section of her bed on which to lie. Her son confirmed this. They both watched a video about adult AD/HD, which included scenes of a disorganized, messy home.

"That's nothing," Jane's son said. "Look, you can still see the floor, and those stacks of stuff are only a foot high!"

Of course, Jane is an extreme example of disorganization. But many people with AD/HD tell tales of lost papers, forgotten meetings, and frustrated spouses and coworkers. Disorganization is a prime side effect of the distractibility that comes with AD/HD. People start projects and get sidetracked. They begin to straighten up and are distracted by the first thing they pick up; they drop what they're doing to do something else, and then they can't remember where they dropped the first thing.

Bill* is an incredibly creative architect with what I would call "moderate" organizational difficulties. He would imagine *and design wonderfully innovative office buildings and stores, but he could not organize himself enough to follow through with the details of putting the designs on paper. His missed deadlines were hurting an otherwise brilliant career.*

There are also many people with AD/HD with only "mild" organizational problems. They tend to function adequately, but usually with a great deal of stress or anxiety. They are frequently late for appointments and often misplace important papers (though they usually find these after some searching). Their disorganization is a source of stress for them and an annoyance for others.

KNOWING VERSUS DOING

These difficulties with organization don't come from a lack of knowing what to do. It's the inability to do what you know you should and could do. That's what makes it so frustrating.

Someone with mild or even moderate AD/HD might improve his or her organizational skills in a particular area of life for a period of time if highly motivated to do so. But can you sustain these organizational skills? This is often where adults with AD/HD fail. You know what you want to do. You may even be able to do it for a short period of time. But for some reason you stop. Now you feel like a failure. Others may view you as lazy, unmotivated, or rebellious because you have already demonstrated that you *can* be better organized, therefore you must not be trying. Most people tolerate those who have an inability to perform at a certain level but get very annoyed with someone who has shown the ability to perform at a certain level on one day and is not performing at the same level the next day.

The inconsistency of organization in the lives of many people with AD/HD often leads to frustration and poor self-esteem.

Inconsistency

This inconsistency puzzles the researchers as well. How can a person's behavior be fine one day and erratic the next?

Dr. Russell A. Barkley, one of the leading AD/HD scholars, notes, "What is not so clear from research is whether this deficit in paying attention reflects a primary deficit in sustained attention or is secondary to the problem of behavioral disinhibition." In other words, does the ability to pay attention just "wear out" after a while, or does the person with AD/HD lose the ability to say no to distractions? Barkley goes on to support the latter view, that *behavioral disinhibition* creates problems for those with AD/HD. This is described as a proneness to be easily led away from the task at hand and not being able to stop oneself from doing "more interesting" activities.

"The most consistent findings," Barkley says, "are for a primary deficit in behavioral or response inhibition, the ability to delay responses, or the tolerance for delay intervals within the tasks. Thus, the primary component of AD/HD is more one of disinhibition or poor delay of responding than inattention."[1]

So the problem is not that the person with AD/HD can't attend to things, but that the person with AD/HD attends to everything! If the current task stops being interesting—if it does not reward the person's attention any longer—then the mind flits off to something else.

There can also be problems with *activation*. With AD/HD, it's hard getting started on a task as well as sustaining energy and staying with a task.

As we said earlier, it is expensive for someone with AD/HD to pay attention. It takes great effort to focus on a particular task, and it takes great effort to sustain that focus. With AD/HD, there is a limit to the effort you can apply to a task before your energy is "spent." This may be a key to attentional inconsistency.

Let's say you worked at a rather sedentary job but suddenly were asked to unload a truck full of heavy crates. No one would blame you for taking it easy the rest of the day. You have expended a lot of energy. Your body is tired.

Similarly, the person with AD/HD may work hard one day to stay "on task," maintaining concentration to get a job done, but that's hard work. The next day, the person's brain may take it easy—may stop working so hard—leaving gaps in the ability to attend to tasks.

THE KEYS TO IMPROVEMENT

Many adults with AD/HD have shelves full of how-to-organize-your-life books. Some buy them for themselves (often as New Year's resolutions), and some receive them as gifts from well-intentioned spouses, friends, or co-workers. Unfortunately, people with AD/HD are frequently unable to focus long enough to read them, or they often forget what they have read, or they start to implement the ideas with all the best intentions but fail to follow through.

No one is more troubled by these tendencies than the

people with AD/HD themselves. You may feel that you are fighting a losing battle.

For that reason, the first key to improving organizational skills is *hope*. The second is *understanding*. First, you need to believe that your life can become more organized—and this is tough after repeated attempts and failures. Second, you need to understand the nature of AD/HD and set reasonable goals at a reasonable pace.

We love the title of one of the early books on AD/HD: *You Mean I'm Not Lazy, Stupid or Crazy?*[2] Those labels can be devastating, and it's important to realize that they're not true. When you have AD/HD, you need to accept yourself for who you truly are. Yes, AD/HD creates some problems for you, but it's not a moral shortcoming. What's more, you can manage these problems. Although it won't be easy, you can take small steps to improve the organization of your life and lessen the negative effects of seemingly inevitable disorganization.

Once you understand the reason for your difficulties and have hope that things can change, you can have renewed energy to tackle the problem.

THE ROLE OF MEDICATION

One of the most obvious ways for someone with AD/HD to improve organizational skills is to take medication. We have seen dramatic changes in the organizational abilities of many adults with AD/HD once they went on medication—especially in those with moderate to severe levels of AD/HD.

Amazingly, it seems that some people with AD/HD don't even recognize their own disorganization. They become so familiar with the stacks of paper and piles of stuff that they stop paying attention to them. Medication can often improve their focus to the point that they notice the surrounding disarray. One client explained, "It wasn't until I took medication that I even saw the mess. My desk was always piled high with papers, and I almost never got my work in on time. That was just normal for me. Once I started medication, I not only saw the mess, but I had the energy and ability to focus on the problem. My desk is clean!"

One friend proudly showed me his desk after he had begun taking medication for AD/HD. It was covered with "only" about two inches of papers. There were papers sticking out of half-open drawers. "At least now I see them!" he exclaimed. "I never even noticed all these papers before!"

The medication had not turned this man into a neat freak. Far from it! But it was giving him the initial focus he needed. Now he could learn how to keep those piles of papers from accumulating.

Despite such glowing testimonials, we need to be clear on several points:

Medication does not solve all the problems. Pills are not skills. People with AD/HD learn bad habits as they live with their disorder. You may not have learned basic organizational strategies because you could never succeed at applying them. Medication can improve your ability to focus, to screen out distractions, but you still have to learn how to organize your life. That's why counseling and coaching play a crucial role. You need to work on your organizational strategies.

Medication does not work for everybody. Studies show that 70 to 80 percent of AD/HD clients show some improvement with medication, but that leaves 20 to 30 percent who don't.

Some improvement may be seen without medication. Those who don't want to take medication can also make some progress by working hard to adopt some of the organizational strategies mentioned below. It will be a tough fight (depending on the level of one's AD/HD), but some improvements are possible.

THE THREE SS

Organizational management for people with AD/HD can be broken into three categories: Self, Space, and Stuff.

Self

Keeping oneself organized is the ultimate challenge for those with AD/HD. You might think the very fact that you have AD/HD makes self-organization impossible. But it can be done. In fact, some people with AD/HD have coped with this disorder by becoming extremely organized. By relying on the routine of organization, they have become able to manage their lives effectively.

Structure. Many find a highly structured environment conducive to getting things done. With an absence of such structure, many get easily distracted by the multiple options available and get nothing important accomplished.

One client, for example, always does the laundry on Monday, goes grocery shopping on Tuesday, and pays bills on Friday. She follows this pattern religiously. If the grocery store were ever closed on Tuesday, she would be thrown off. She feels that if she adjusts her schedule she would be too distracted to get her tasks completed.

Priorities. Establishing priorities is extremely important. Unfortunately, those with AD/HD find this very difficult to do. Earlier we mentioned the difficulty in "weighing" things in the mind. For the person with AD/HD, many items entertain the brain as equally attractive options. In the midst of trying to write a term paper for college or finish a business report, a phone call to a friend may claim equal importance.

It is helpful to keep in mind the slogan "First things first." The person with AD/HD will not naturally rate things according to priority. The AD/HD brain does not know what "first things" to put first. But you can establish a habit of intentionally rating the priority of tasks. Maybe it becomes a routine at the beginning of the day; you make a list and select the three most important tasks in order. Then make it a point to put first things first. (It may be helpful to ask others for input as you begin to learn to prioritize.)

Small steps. Although many with AD/HD have read about, heard lectures about, or attended workshops on time management, many fail to put the recommendations into action. Often they put down the book or come home from the workshop and determine to change their lives radically. Everything must go! Old habits will be swept out and new habits adopted.

How long does your determination last? A day? A week? Do you become frustrated because you are trying to do too much? Have you set impossible goals for yourself? Are you expecting to create overnight life changes that would reasonably take a year or two, and maybe longer for those struggling with AD/HD?

It's better to choose one thing, just one small step you can work on, over the next two months. Then try another step. Then another. In a year you will have taken five or six positive steps toward a better life. That's far better than crashing and burning in the first week.

In the movie *What About Bob?*, Bill Murray plays a man dealing with emotional problems. Bob is told that he must not try to recover all at once, that he must take "baby steps"—and we see him walking out of the office, putting one foot in front of the other, edging his way forward. It's a funny scene, and a poignant one. As an old Chinese saying goes, "Every journey begins with just one step."

Coping aids. Find a system to remember appointments and obligations. This is critical in our demanding society. How can you juggle the assignments you have from work or school, your responsibilities with children or other family members, social activities, lunch or dinner get-togethers, medical appointments, and so on? Write it all down and then get into the habit of referring to your appointment book. Many people use some type of weekly or monthly calendar with a "to-do" list. This can be especially helpful if important long-term goals and steps to accomplish such goals are included. Or, if these options are impossible for you, find some other system that works.

Many adults with AD/HD use their creativity to cope with their disorganized lives. One of the most creative coping methods we've seen was used by a client who had severe AD/HD and was unable to follow a schedule. This was especially difficult for him because he was in the sales business, which required him to attend to various meetings on a regular basis.

He was charming, personable, well-liked, and did an excellent job—when he remembered to show up for appointments. But, of course, his erratic attendance was a major problem.

He had tried numerous time management schedule books. Only he would lose them. Or he would forget to look at his schedule. He was at his wits' end. As a creative alternative, he began to wear a beeper. The office would call and tell him when and where to go next. That way he didn't need to follow a schedule. That system worked quite well for him—as long as he remembered to wear the beeper!

Obviously, time management is also a problem for some people without AD/HD, but the problem is entirely different for the person who has it. Time in general seems to be somewhat elusive. It's an abstract concept, separated from their daily lives. Time seems indefinite, infinite, and unable to be sliced into neat one-hour components. When you are beginning to use a calendar, it can be challenging. Remember to break a long-term project into small, manageable steps and write those into your schedule.

Once I (Michele) asked a client to do a five- to ten-minute presentation on his experiences with AD/HD. After fifteen minutes I had to interrupt him because he kept on talking with no sign of abating. This in itself was an instructive moment: He commented that it was ridiculous to give a person with AD/HD a five- to ten-minute time frame, because he had no sense of time!

Allow time each day to organize your next day. Many waste a great deal of time because they fail to plan. Of course this is good advice for anyone, but for those with

AD/HD, it's a necessity. Too many attractive distractions await those with AD/HD. Unless you have a track to follow, you will certainly get lost.

Stores are full of new items designed to help organize your time. There are numerous calendars, to-do lists, address books, and note organizers for computers, Palm Pilots, and your desktop.

There are also beeping and vibrating watches with multiple time settings, and voice recordings to prompt you. There are answering machines with a "memo" function for you to record messages to yourself. There are even key chains with mini-recorders enclosed, so you can record things you don't want to forget.

Take time to explore the technological advances available to see if you find something that may be helpful for you.

Procrastination. Procrastination has many root causes. For some people, it's a desire for perfection, a fear of failure, or an unconscious desire to sabotage one's own work. A person with AD/HD, however, procrastinates for different reasons—a difficulty understanding the reality of time, the "expensiveness" of sustained attention, and the lack of "activation" for new efforts.

If this is a problem for you, we bring you a simple message: *Decrease procrastination today!*

We're not going to tell you to stop procrastinating entirely, because we're sure you've heard that before, tried that before, and failed too many times. So, for now, just try to procrastinate *less*. And you can start tomorrow. (Just kidding. You need to start today.)

If you usually wait to begin a work project or school assignment until the night before it's due, try to begin the day before. Remember, success is often measured by small steps.

Hopefully someday you will put an end to your procrastination. Someday. But today you can do one small thing to decrease it.

Space

Space . . . the final frontier. No, not that kind of space. There's plenty of that. We're talking about a very limited space. The space on top of your desk. The space in your file cabinet. Or the space in your closet. There never seems to be enough space to store all the stuff we think we need. Part of getting organized is using the finite space we have more efficiently.

Everything has a home. To function in a fairly anxiety-free state, you need to have a place for most things. It will help simplify matters if you learn to keep certain items in certain places.

To do this, you need to establish a routine for the use of your space. For example, when you come home, place your keys on the key hook by the door. Once this becomes established as a habit, it will eliminate the morning stress of "Where are my keys? I'm going to be late!" The key hook will become the home for keys.

The same principle can work for papers. Bills, and only bills, could go into a basket on the kitchen counter. Other forms of paperwork, things that require some action other than payment, could be placed into a file or slot holder, whereas papers that you just wish to read at your leisure could be in a second file or slot, and items to file could be placed into a third file or slot.

This type of rough sorting would enable you to keep track of the important papers in your life. In the office, a similar type of rough sorting system could be developed.

Storage containers. Use of files and a file cabinet or file storage container is also extremely helpful for those who struggle with organization. There are numerous storage containers available in office supply stores. It is well worth a trip to wander through the store and see what type of storage systems may work to simplify your particular organizational needs.

Storage containers work because they get things out of your way. A file will not distract you, and it will not clutter your space if it's sitting in a cabinet somewhere. Proper labeling of file drawers or boxes will help you retrieve files when you need them.

Space is finite, stuff is not. Deal with the reality of space. It is important to realize the limits of space when you make decisions of what to keep and what to discard. Although it may be useful someday to look up an article from a magazine from ten years ago, it is unlikely you will remember where you saw the article, and even more unlikely that you would be able to retrieve the article when you need it. A local library would be a much better resource for finding such information. How many people do you know who have saved years' worth of certain magazines, hoping to use them someday, but never touch them again?

Periodically review the items taking up space and make sure they are still important enough to deserve the space they take up. Don't hesitate to throw things away or donate them to a thrift store. Think in terms of each item "paying rent" for the space it uses up. Does its value to you make up for the "rent" it has to pay?

Some homes do an annual "spring cleaning" in which unneeded "junk" is discarded or sold in a yard sale (to clutter someone else's space for a while). You might want to establish a regular evaluation of stuff and space. Less stuff is easier to manage.

Stuff

Obviously, our space is often cluttered because we have too much stuff in it. Therefore space management goes hand in hand with stuff management. People with AD/HD tend to be pack rats, collecting things they may use someday. It's that same "can't say no" principle. Some people can't say no to an impulse or distraction, others can't say no to a cute piece of junk in their basement because of the endless creative possibilities associated with it.

Spend fifteen minutes a day decreasing clutter. Make time each day or at least each week to organize your stuff. It would be great if your piles of paper would learn to organize themselves, but that won't happen. The longer you delay, the larger those piles will become.

But here's the secret: You don't have to clear the whole pile all at once. Just stay a step ahead of the stuff. Most people accumulate about ten minutes worth of stuff (junk mail, unneeded objects, magazines they'll never read, etc.) a day. That is, it would take about ten minutes each day to deal with each day's new stuff. If you devote just fifteen minutes each day to organizing the stuff you have accumulated, you'll chip away at those piles. In a week or two, you may even see the surface of your desk.

"But I don't have fifteen minutes a day!"

We hear you. But consider how much time you spend looking for stuff each day. Consider the anxiety that search creates, not to mention the family conflict, late fees from overdue bills, or missed deadlines. You've got that fifteen minutes a day, you just have to harness it.

Use bright colors or enticing designs. It may be easier and more enticing to work with your stuff if you use bright colors and/or interesting containers. Use files of different colors for different types of papers—work is orange, home is yellow, bills are red, and so on.

Cut down on your reading material. Many people with AD/HD have stacks of magazines and newspapers they haven't read. They intend to read them someday, but they probably won't.

If that's the case with you, cut off this problem at the source. Cancel some subscriptions. If you get a daily newspaper, maybe you'd be all right with Sunday only. If you get several magazines, think about which ones you really need (or really read). Why couldn't you go to a library once a month to read the others?

▼

Monitor your use of book, CD, or video clubs. Often those cards don't get sent back and the products come whether you want them or not. Then they just add to your clutter. It might be best to drop out of the club and go to a store for what you really want.

Make a list before you shop. On impulse, people with AD/HD often buy things they don't need. Then the stuff sits around collecting dust, but you don't want to throw it out because you spent good money on it.

Make a shopping list before you shop—and stick to it. That will help to keep you from filling your home with white elephants.

Handle papers no more than twice. Some success experts tell executives to handle papers once. That is, they should decide on each thing immediately and pass it on for appropriate action. That's not bad advice for any of us, though we might need a second chance to decide what to do with something. Many people with AD/HD have piles of papers they've looked at again and again and again. By the second time, file it or toss it!

Use those sticky memo notes. (Have a supply handy.) If you are putting papers in a pile "for future consideration," make sure each one has a note on it saying what needs to be done or decided. That way you won't need to reread all those papers, and you can get rid of them faster.

Give yourself a "throwaway budget." Some people hang on to major pieces of junk because they feel these pieces are worth something. An old toaster. That Veg-o-matic in the closet. An old Commodore computer. And maybe someday these things will come in handy, right?!

Here's an idea. Ask yourself, "How much is it worth to have an uncluttered environment?" Set a dollar figure on that. Five hundred dollars? A thousand? In terms of your peace of mind, and the efficiency of your life, how much is that worth to you?

Write that figure down at the top of a piece of paper. That's your "throwaway budget." Then start looking at your old junk. If you threw away your toaster and decided down the road that you needed a new one, how much would one cost? Write that down and subtract it from your "budget" figure. How much would a new Veg-o-matic cost you if you needed one? Subtract that, too. And so on.

You probably don't really need to set aside that money, because you'll probably never need to replace those old objects. But in your mind, you're putting a value on an uncluttered home and charging the replacement cost of your old junk against it. Which is really more important to you? That may give you the push you need to toss that junk or donate it to a worthy cause.

In summary, people with AD/HD often need to learn basic organizational skills. You may have tried various methods in the past and failed. But now that you know about AD/HD, you can cut yourself some slack and allow yourself a little more time to develop those organizational habits. If you are now on medication, you should also have a renewed focus that will help you apply those organizational methods.

It is important to try again. Don't be discouraged if you are not successful on your first few tries. Disorganization may have become a habit for you, but habits can be changed—one small step at a time.

▼

Just the Facts

▶ It is not a lack of knowing what to do that causes people with AD/HD difficulty with organization. It is the inability to do what they know they should and could do.

▶ The inconsistent ability to remain organized and perform tasks creates much frustration and leads to poor self-esteem for many adults with AD/HD.

▶ There are many specific ways of organizing your self, space, and stuff, including:

Self

▶ Structure your environment/routine
▶ Practice prioritizing—first things first
▶ Break tasks into small steps and be realistic about the pace for change
▶ Devise a creative system to remember appointments and obligations
▶ Allow time to plan your day in advance
▶ Procrastinate less

Space

▶ Identify specific places for important items (keys, bills, etc.)
▶ Use functional storage containers
▶ Regularly evaluate the immediate value of the stuff taking up your limited space
▶ Don't hesitate to throw away or donate stuff from time to time

More Facts

Stuff

► Take fifteen minutes each day to decrease clutter
► Use bright colors and interesting containers
► Cut down on your reading material
► Make a list before you shop
► Handle papers no more than twice
► Ask yourself, "How much is it worth to have an uncluttered environment?" and give yourself a "throwaway budget"

NOTES

1. From the video *AD/HD in Adults* and the accompanying program manual *AD/HD in Adults* (New York: Guilford Press, 1994).
2. Kate Kelly and Peggy Ramundo, *You Mean I'm Not Lazy, Stupid or Crazy?* (Cincinnati: Tyrell and Jerem Press, 1993).

RESOURCE

National Association of Professional Organizers
1033 La Posada Drive
Austin, TX 78752
512-206-0151

CHAPTER SIXTEEN

LEARNING

ANDREW* WAS CLEARLY NOT WORKING UP TO HIS POTENTIAL. *He had great promise, yet he had flunked out of two colleges. He seemed very smart, but somehow he just couldn't apply himself to college tasks.*

In frustration, Andrew saw a counselor, who suspected AD/HD and sent him for an evaluation. Andrew was, in fact, diagnosed with AD/HD. Treatment involved medication as well as counseling and education for Andrew and his family.

Now Andrew is doing well in his second semester in college. The treatment didn't make his AD/HD go away, but it gave him the push he needed to get ahead of it. He still needs to structure his time more than most college students do, but he has learned how to do this. For instance, he goes to the library every Monday night to study—every Monday night, without fail. He knows that if he skips a Monday study time, he probably won't make it up.

Andrew has also learned to break down his assignments into pieces and plan a schedule that gives him time to do each piece. He also takes his language lab independently, so he can replay a session if needed and go at his own pace.

In addition, Andrew continues in counseling. He has been

working through many issues related to his self-esteem and interpersonal relationships.

AD/HD can make learning difficult. If you are very bright, you may not have difficulties until high school or college, when you finally need to access your full brainpower. At that point, many drop out of school or switch to less challenging schools or courses. Since AD/HD affects the information a person takes in, it has a drastic impact on the ability to learn.

WHAT IS LEARNING?

There are many tasks involved in the learning process. First, a person takes in information, usually by hearing or seeing a presentation of the material.

Second, a person sifts through the information received, keeping that which is important and allowing the rest to be forgotten. This aspect of learning is often overlooked, but "selective forgetting" is actually a key part of the process. If we didn't do this, we would be overwhelmed with the amount of data we receive.

Third, a person retains the important information. Short-term memory happens naturally, while long-term memory may involve some effort at memorizing the material.

Finally, a person retrieves the information at the appropriate time. Many of us have had the embarrassing experience of knowing that we know something—a person's name, for instance—but not being able to recall it. In such cases, the information is actually there, stored somewhere in our brains, but the neural signposts leading us to its location have faded.

AD/HD can cause difficulty in any or all of these aspects of the learning process.

Taking In Information

The first problem someone with AD/HD has is simply receiving information. Because of fluctuations in attention span, a lot of data never gets into the brain at all. The person with AD/HD is frequently distracted by other noises, movements, even thoughts. Competing noises or thoughts seem equally attractive to the brain, so it's hard to filter out distractions and gather the important information being presented.

A person with AD/HD has special difficulty attending to *auditory information*—lectures, seminars, verbal directions, and so on. Visual stimuli are more attractive, easier to follow.

As we have already indicated, AD/HD can fill a person's life with gaps—we've called them "blinks"—and so he or she will tend to get only part of the information presented.

Those with AD/HD also have difficulty *listening and taking notes* at the same time, as in a lecture or seminar situation. Many people take this ability for granted, but it requires regular shifting of attention from the lecture to the paper and back again. Every shift is a potential off-ramp on the information highway. Tasks that require divided attention are usually quite hard for people with AD/HD.

Many adults with AD/HD also have trouble *reading*. Some of this may stem from early school experiences. Often a child who falls behind early in reading skills—due to AD/HD or some other learning problem—feels he or she is always playing catch-up.

But reading can also be a less rewarding activity than watching something or even listening—especially if you're reading textbooks. Remember how much effort it takes for someone with AD/HD to pay attention. With reading, there is no visual movement or ongoing sound to help draw the person's attention to the material—just the words on the page. It takes extra energy to read and extra motivation to even start a reading assignment.

Reading also requires a certain amount of consistent mental participation—visualizing or reframing the material one reads. But this is, in a way, a split task—reading and visualizing, reading and visualizing—and the reader can get lost in the transitions. We've heard many people with AD/HD talk about reading and rereading the same page and not being able to get through it. It's not that the information is too heavy for them; it's just that their minds go off on other journeys before they finish the page.

Reading takes a long time. It requires sustained attention, something that's very difficult for the person with AD/HD. And in many situations, reading is progressive. That is, page 47 is based on things you've read on page 46, and so on. If you "blink" on page 46 (perhaps not even realizing it), you will have a hard time understanding page 47 and beyond.

All of these factors make reading an especially challenging task for those with AD/HD. And, since reading is fundamental to education, this creates learning problems for many.

There's one other setback in the process of taking in information—*emotional self-talk*. As we have seen, people with AD/HD face great difficulty in this first aspect of learning, and therefore the whole process is fraught with anxiety.

"Can I do this? Maybe not. Probably not. And what will happen if I don't?"

Most people can just pick up a book and read, or sit down at a lecture and takes notes. But the person with AD/HD has a whole emotional monologue going on, and this can be a source of distraction. It's like having a second television on in the same room.

Because many people with AD/HD have poor self-esteem, this emotional monologue is usually negative: "I'll never be able to do this." This often becomes a self-fulfilling prophecy.

Psychologist Albert Ellis talks about the process of "awfulizing"—making a situation more awful than it really is by imagining all sorts of disasters. "I can't read this, and because I can't, I'll flunk out of school, and then I'll only be able to get a fast-food job flipping burgers, so I won't ever be able to buy a house. . . . " So, while you should be on page 47, your mind is on skid row somewhere, collecting unemployment checks.

In a few cases, even positive self-talk can be a distraction. "Hey, I'm doing pretty well. I'm following this lecture perfectly. If I keep this up, I'll be able to go on for a Master's degree, and maybe teach in some comfy community college and . . . " And you've lost it again.

The point is that learning is an issue for those with AD/HD, and the emotional response to this issue can take center stage in one's mind, making it even more difficult to learn.

Sifting Through Information

AD/HD also makes it hard to decide what is important and what is not. People without AD/HD regularly weigh the merits of the information they receive, but people with AD/HD often say yes to everything. It all comes in and it all gets equal billing.

Let's say two college students go to the same lecture. The first, who has AD/HD, listens to the speaker but also hears someone coughing in the back row. The other one, without AD/HD, hears the coughing too, but quickly decides, "Oh, that's just someone with a bad cold. It's more important to listen to the lecture." The student with AD/HD, however, gives equal weight to the cougher and the professor. Add seven other background noises, and that student has a lot to contend with.

Helen tells of her attempts to listen to college lectures in the days before she got treatment for AD/HD. "I would count the number of tiles in the ceiling, the number of red shirts in the room, the number of steps in the lecture hall." Every detail clamored for her attention.

Most people routinely sift important information from unimportant, even when it comes from the same source, but people with AD/HD don't do this well. The lecturer may tell an amusing legend about how Euclid came up with a certain theorem. The student without AD/HD knows that the story is just a story — the important thing is the theorem. But the AD/HD student takes it all in, placing just as much value on the color of Euclid's toga as on the variables in his equations.

That might be fine if a person could remember all of it and instantly access any detail needed. But we can only hold so many details in our brains, and it's confusing to sift through a lot of trivia to get to the important stuff. Ironically, the learning problem of the student with AD/HD is not getting too little information, but getting too much!

In other words, when you have AD/HD, your brain can be a lot like your home or office—cluttered. If you took every piece of mail you've received in the last year and just piled it all on your desk, how would you ever find the important things? Most people learn to throw out the junk right away so it doesn't clutter their desks. Similarly, they sift out the unimportant information they receive so it doesn't clutter their brains. But people with AD/HD have trouble throwing things away, whether it's junk mail or "junk data."

As a result, you often feel overloaded. There is too much to deal with, so you just shut down. At that point, you miss out on important new information because you've been overloaded by unimportant details.

Retaining the Important Information

People with AD/HD often have trouble storing information. Even though they may hear or see the information, it may not get to their short- or long-term memory. Because the data is not sifted, there is too much to handle and the memory quickly fills up. It's something like a computer whose memory gets packed with video games. When you have an important file to save, you get an "out of memory" message.

Everyone's memory fades through time. A person may recall an event that happened years earlier but may remember only its high points—the most important details. However, when you have AD/HD, your memories are not that well organized. You might remember the color of the tie your boss wore on the day you got your job, but you might forget some key details of your job.

Retrieving Information

Like someone searching for a birth certificate in a pile of store fliers and magazine promotions, the person with AD/HD may have a hard time retrieving something that has been learned. This is one of the more embarrassing aspects of AD/HD. It can earn you a label of "absent-minded," "airhead," "space cadet," or something worse.

This is especially frustrating when you've expended so much effort to learn the material in the first place. When you study for an exam every night for a week, you want that effort to pay off. Sadly, for many with AD/HD, it doesn't. Regularly our AD/HD clients tell us they have to study three or four times as much as their classmates, and still they struggle.

It's a bit like pouring water into a cup with a narrow opening at the top and a crack in the bottom. Even when you succeed, with great effort, in pouring water in, it leaks out. The cup is not doing its job. In the same way, the AD/HD brain is not only making it difficult to get information in, it is also letting it leak out.

Organizational Difficulties

Many people with AD/HD have difficulty organizing their lives. This can hinder the learning process significantly, in many different ways.

For one thing, people with AD/HD often lose things. And if you can't find your lists, keys, supplies, and so on, it sets you back. How can you finish that research paper when you wrote the first three pages on a computer disk you can't locate?

Since time management is also a struggle for those with AD/HD, you might often run late for appointments or meetings—or forget about them entirely. Or you might realize at 11 P.M. Monday that an assignment is due for Tuesday's 8 A.M. class.

Certainly there are many without AD/HD who are also disorganized and poor time managers. But when you have AD/HD, you have so many other factors working against you that missing a class or a project could be disastrous. It is tough to play catch-up all the time.

We should also note that organizational difficulties aren't always a problem for those with AD/HD. And we've known some with AD/HD who have worked hard to organize their lives and succeeded at it.

Learning Disabilities

Sometimes a person will have a specific learning disability in addition to AD/HD. But wait! Isn't AD/HD a learning disability itself? Not technically. There are strong relationships between AD/HD and learning disabilities, but AD/HD itself has not been classified in that category.

A learning disability is a psychological disorder that has to do with "using language, spoken or written, which may manifest itself in an imperfect ability to listen, think, speak, read, write, spell, or do mathematical calculations. The term includes such conditions as perceptual handicaps, brain injury, minimal brain dysfunction, dyslexia, and developmental aphasia."[1]

So there may be other learning problems that follow someone with AD/HD through childhood and into adulthood. Dr. Larry Silver states, "Of all the children and adolescents with AD/HD, it is estimated that between 50% and 80% will also have a learning disability."[2]

An excellent resource for information on learning

disabilities is *www.ldonline.com* and the Learning Disability Association, 4156 Library Road, Pittsburgh, PA 15234.

Tips for Learning Better

Schools are now required by federal law to offer specialized help for students with AD/HD and/or learning disabilities. But there are several strategies mentioned here to help keep the person with AD/HD on track in a learning environment.

1. *Tape your classes, lectures, or seminars.* Then you can replay the tape later to fill in any gaps. If you use a tape recorder with a counter, just write down the number when you realize you've missed something to help you more easily locate specific material.

2. *Get notes from someone else.* Classmates, friends, coworkers, professors, or speakers may be able to supply you with notes so that you can listen without the distraction of taking notes yourself. If you explain your AD/HD, they should be happy to accommodate you—you're not being lazy, you're being smart.

3. *Use a study group or tutor.* You need help differentiating important from unimportant information. Others can help you with this. Even if it's not an organized study group or tutoring

session, try to review the content of the class or seminar with others.

4. Use medication. Even those who resist taking medication on a full-time basis find that it can help greatly in learning situations. You could plan "medicated mornings" and schedule your classes (or toughest work projects) for the times when the medication is having its fullest effect.

5. Establish accountability. Since motivation is often a problem for someone with AD/HD, get someone to check on you periodically, just to make sure you are doing what you said you wanted to be doing. A peer or a coach can help.

6. Get counseling. A counselor can teach you new strategies and skills, help repair your self-esteem, and reduce your negative self-talk.

ACCOMMODATIONS FOR THE PERSON WITH AD/HD

Employers, teachers, and administrators can make "reasonable accommodations" for AD/HD that can help immensely. Remember that people with AD/HD are not dumb. They just have difficulty with the normal pace and style of gathering information. The following measures may help get around that.

▶ Make notes available for meetings or classes.
▶ Repeat the key points of a lecture or meeting.

▶ Give all assignments in written form, not just orally.
▶ Set intermediate deadlines so that part of the project should be done by this date, the next part by that date, and so on.
▶ Allow for alternative testing, including essay tests, oral reports, or skills tests. Normal written tests do not always fairly assess the knowledge of a student with AD/HD.
▶ Allow untimed tests. Students with AD/HD may take longer to summon the information, but it's there.
▶ Take stand-up, walk-around breaks in classes or meetings. (In business, try short stand-up meetings.)

—— Just the Facts ——

▶ People with AD/HD often have learning difficulties in the following areas:
  • Taking in information
  • Sifting through information
  • Retaining the important information
  • Retrieving information
  • Organizational difficulties that affect the learning process
  • Possible additional learning disabilities
▶ A person with AD/HD can take responsibility to tape meetings or classes, get notes from others, use a tutor, and seek treatment for AD/HD with medication and counseling.
▶ Companies, teachers, and schools can make certain accommodations for those with AD/HD to make the best use of their potential and overcome some learning problems.

NOTES

1. Federal Law: Education for All Handicapped Children (Public Law 94-142), cited in Larry Silver, *Dr. Larry Silver's Advice to Parents on Attention Deficit Hyperactivity Disorder* (Washington, D.C.: American Psychiatric Press, Inc., 1993), p. 42.
2. Silver, p. 8.

CHAPTER SEVENTEEN

RELATIONSHIPS

PAUL AND MARCY GOT MARRIED ABOUT TEN YEARS AGO. IT WAS Paul's third marriage, Marcy's first. They met, fell in love, and married within just a few months. Marcy was elated— but she didn't know this had been a pattern for Paul's previous relationships. He would dive impulsively into a relationship but soon grow bored.

The difference with this marriage, however, was the fact that they had a child fairly quickly, and then another, and another. Now, even though they both are openly dissatisfied with the relationship, they stay together, primarily because of their three children.

According to Marcy, Paul tends to be very self-centered. He has a difficult time understanding other people's perceptions and can't follow conversations that involve more than one person at a time. He doesn't seem to pick up on social nuances and can only focus on one thing at a time. Therefore, the focus is usually on himself.

This self-focus is a blind spot for Paul, and a chief complaint for Marcy. She sees his selfishness as deliberate. She gets frustrated explaining to him what she expects from him and what needs to be done around the house, yet there never seems

*to be any change for the better. "It's like having a fourth child,"
Marcy explains. "I know he's not stupid, and yet he just doesn't
get it. He's frequently late, insensitive when we're with others,
and he rarely does anything to help around the house." It is
hard for her to fight her feelings of resentment toward him.*

*According to Paul, he's not the problem—Marcy is just too
critical and doesn't understand him. He is oblivious to what
he is doing wrong but admits to being somewhat disorganized. Paul feels that the marriage is in a rut and holds out
little hope that it will ever change. He admits that he is bored
with the relationship but says that he'll stay around as long as
the kids are in the home.*

*Paul also looks for excitement in other activities and hob-
bies. His pattern is to get very involved in a new activity and
impulsively pursue it, only to abandon it and move on to
something else within a few months. For example, he got
interested in photography and bought scads of expensive
equipment. About six months later, he lost interest. Now all
of the stuff lies on a shelf collecting dust.*

Yes, Paul has AD/HD.

Problems in relationships abound when you have
AD/HD. The specific type of problem can vary, depending
on what type of AD/HD you have. Some people with
AD/HD are impulsive and hyperactive, others distracted.
So some of the following descriptions will fit you to a T;
others will sound completely foreign.

"OF COURSE I'M LISTENING"

One common complaint of people with AD/HD is their
apparent difficulty in listening to others. Blame it on their

distractibility, their impulsiveness, or their overactivity, but no matter how you slice it, people with AD/HD find it hard to stay with a conversation. This may not be apparent at first, because new acquaintances are always a little more interesting, and that newness helps to hold your attention. But once a real relationship sets in, watch out—that's when someone with AD/HD may become bored, distracted, and aloof.

People with AD/HD will commonly fidget while someone else is talking, interrupt in the middle of a crucial point, or change the subject abruptly. In some cases, they'll just walk away from a conversation.

Obviously, this can hurt any significant relationship. The difficulty is most apparent in relationships with other adults or older teenagers, since these tend to be more intense and complex than interactions with children.

One father with AD/HD explained it this way: "When my children were little, I could get on the floor with them and play. Their attention spans were short and so was mine. It made for a fun time. But now my kids are older. They want to talk about their music, their MTV, their boyfriends or girlfriends, and their problems. I have a real hard time listening well to any of it. Relationships that were once above average are now nonexistent."

In adult encounters, people with AD/HD are at a tremendous disadvantage. They generally don't pick up subtle nuances, have difficulty following extended or complicated conversations, and may not be interested in the things others want to talk about. It's true that many people have trouble being good conversationalists, whether they have AD/HD or not. But people with AD/HD have to work especially hard at listening.

"HERE TODAY, GONE TOMORROW"

The impulsiveness of AD/HD is well documented. We saw this in the story of Paul and Marcy at the beginning of this chapter. Paul jumped impulsively into the relationship (as was his pattern) and then lost interest after a while. He had the same tendency with his hobbies and his jobs.

Dating a person with AD/HD can be a roller-coaster experience. He or she may seem very interested in pursuing you one day and then be gone the next. The interest might even return later, and vanish again, and return, and so on. This can lead to a frustrating and unhealthy relationship, especially if the non-AD/HD partner goes to great lengths to "win over" the one with AD/HD. The fact is, when you have AD/HD, you're not *playing* hard to get; you *are* hard to get. A marriage can be the same way.

One woman explained: "When we were dating it was great because he was so intense and so exciting. I felt like life was one big adventure with Jack. I never knew what was coming next — camping, the theater, skydiving. He was so unpredictable. But then, as the relationship settled down, I felt like he was bored with me, and jumping on to something else. Our relationship was built on doing things and having fun. But when it came to having a meaningful dialogue, Jack wasn't there. Now, after four years of marriage and a child, Jack has moved on to more exciting pursuits."

Cynics might say that most men and some women are like this anyway. That may be true. But the impulsive person with AD/HD has a special problem in this area. Research indicates that people with AD/HD have a higher rate of divorce, substance abuse, and relational problems. They may also be more prone to affairs, irresponsible risk-taking, and self-destructive behaviors. All of these may be a result of their search for something new and more exciting.

Remember that AD/HD inhibits the ability to say no. That may help the person with AD/HD say yes to a relationship (or other pursuit) too quickly, and then quickly say yes to another new relationship (or another pursuit).

Spouses of those with AD/HD, like Marcy, may feel rejected, and understandably so. Realize the person with AD/HD is not actually rejecting the current relationship, but rather accepting other pursuits that seem to "cost" less. Sustained attention is expensive for the person with AD/HD. It takes a lot of effort to make a marriage work. Of course, this part of AD/HD is no excuse for abandoning one's commitments and responsibilities!

"I Never Said That!"

Forgetfulness is another frequent complaint about AD/HD. This tendency can be the result of several AD/HD symptoms—distractibility, poor listening skills, lack of organization—or of weak memory skills.

This trait can be a great source of tension in relationships. Lateness or missed appointments can create resentment. "Things-to-do" lists get lost or ignored, and arguments break out over "I never said that" or "I never agreed to do that." The person with AD/HD frequently seems to be a day late and a dollar short.

Other people often assume that the person with AD/HD is deliberately lying or trying to squeeze out of a sticky situation. But after the scene is played out again and again, the other person may begin to wonder, "Is it me?" The AD/HD partner can sound so convinced and sure of himself that it seems as if it must be someone else's fault.

The truth is, of course, that people with AD/HD often don't remember. They may have spent ten minutes going over the shopping list, but that may have been a "blink," a time of distraction, and none of it stuck.

This pattern will continue to cause problems unless the person acknowledges his or her memory weakness and others arrive at an understanding of the problem. They need to act without judgment, and the one with AD/HD needs to act without pride. This way, "I never said that" can become "Did I say that?" And that can lead to "You must have forgotten. How can we help you remember next time?" When you have AD/HD, you need to work together with the people in your life to find ways to organize information and establish regular reminders.

If you have AD/HD, one suggestion that helps is to always repeat what you heard before going off to follow directions. Or when giving directions to persons with AD/HD, ask them to repeat what they heard.

"GET OFF MY CASE!"

Many people with AD/HD are playing a game of subtle deception. They can get quite good at it. But trying to maintain that you have it together when you know you don't can be a source of tremendous pain. I've seen many who medicate their pain with alcohol, others who retreat from any emotional intimacy, and still others who flare up in a defensive rage when they are challenged.

The pain of such people is usually just below the surface, so anyone who pricks the skin at all may find a deep level of anger and frustration. Relationships may be characterized by heated arguments or by walls of avoidance. Any comment may be a battlefield, or else people are walking away from each other whenever they feel even the slightest pressure or challenge. You may be spitting fire at each other, or you may go through life feeling like you're walking on eggshells, not wanting to awaken the monster within.

When Marilyn first married Sam, she was drawn to his assertive confidence and apparent strength. But as she got closer, she found a man who could not stand to have anyone question him or challenge his thinking. Sam was trying to run several projects at once and would jump from thing to thing. At first Marilyn marveled at how he seemed to handle it all. But then she learned the truth. He was not handling it. His money and business were really just a shell game—he was pretending to be someone he wasn't, pretending to have something that he didn't.

She loved him and wanted to support him, but when she tried to talk to him about it, he would deny that there was a problem and just walk away. If she pursued him, he became angry and sometimes violent. Over time Marilyn learned to let him go but lived with the frustration of not being able to get close to him. She stood by and watched as Sam became more and more frustrated, more and more angry, and increasingly isolated. Marilyn simply learned how to get out of his way.

The problem with AD/HD-induced anger in relationships, whether openly expressed or hidden, is that the person with AD/HD isn't really angry with the spouse or friend. In the heat of the moment it may seem that way, but the person is really angry at *it*—at the AD/HD. The spouse or friend feels helpless and can respond in anger at being unfairly blamed.

When the anger is "stuffed" and not expressed, it festers. It can paralyze a relationship. Counseling can be crucial for a couple whose relationship has stagnated (or exploded) due to anger at AD/HD. Both parties need a safe environment to express their frustrations honestly and healthily. The monster can be tamed.

"ALL ABOUT ME"

People with AD/HD tend to be more self-focused than others. Some would interpret this behavior as selfish, but there's a moral judgment in that term that doesn't always apply.

As we have said, AD/HD makes it difficult to sustain attention toward outside objects. It is expensive to pay attention, and that "expense" is hard to pay unless there are specific "rewards." What kind of rewards? Entertainment, excitement, interest, novelty.

Picture the couch potato watching TV with the remote control in hand. When a show stops giving him anything new and exciting, he flicks to a different channel. If he finds a show on, say, basket-weaving in Uganda, he will move quickly past it—unless he happens to be a basket-weaver or unless he's from Uganda. We all find things that pertain to ourselves more interesting than things that don't. With AD/HD, we can say those experiences, conversations, and people that focus on your particular interests and needs "pay off" — the attention is rewarded.

All of us are generally more interested in things that have to do with our own lives than in things outside our experience. But AD/HD creates a greater imbalance in this area. It is much harder to pay attention to things outside the self and, comparatively, much easier to attend to self-related things. Therefore, the person with AD/HD is more self-focused and can seem selfish to others.

A woman described her AD/HD husband this way: "He will sit and watch TV and never help out around the house unless I badger him. He forgets to take out the trash or to do any of the chores I ask him to do. He frequently will not show up or will be late to appointments that I make for us, like parent-teacher conferences or doctor's appointments for the kids. But he never seems to forget about the hunting trip with the guys or any trips he's interested in!"

Most people have an understanding of delayed gratification. Today's trip to the dentist may be painful, but we know that it will create long-term dental health—and so it's worth it. We don't like to do dishes, but we know that they'll just pile up until they get washed, and it's much easier to wash dishes before they get encrusted. We may not enjoy hearing all the details of the story Mrs. Oshkosh is telling us, but we know that she'll be offended if we don't listen—and we don't want to risk the wrath of Mrs. Oshkosh!

But the person with AD/HD lives in the moment. That long-term view is often not available. So the dishes will pile up and crust over and the person will buy paper plates. But that does not mean the person with AD/HD is selfish, just self-focused and moment-to-moment.

Of course, this behavior can wreak havoc in relationships. Good relationships are built on relatively equal participation, and if one partner feels that he or she is putting in way more than 50 percent of the effort, resentment can grow. People need to insist on responsible participation by those with AD/HD. Working with the strengths of the person with AD/HD and working out compromises can be a relationship-saving strategy.

"IT'S ALL MY FAULT"

Many people with AD/HD are plagued with a poor self-image, usually as a result of years of underachievement and misunderstanding. Many have struggled through school, feeling dumb and lazy. Teachers, parents, bosses, spouses, and peers often reinforce these labels.

In relationships, this poor self-image comes through in many ways, including insecurity, lack of confidence, overcompensation, and avoidance.

People with AD/HD often seek jobs in occupations that are beneath them, desperately trying to avoid failure by lowering the stakes. They may do the same in dating relationships, dating "beneath themselves" in order to feel more competent. These relationships frequently self-destruct in time, only to be repeated again because the root issues are still there. We have seen this trait especially in women.

Andrea had a history of dating men who were all wrong for

her. She was a very poor student and in high school got into the wrong crowd, experimenting with drugs, sex, and alcohol. After high school, she meandered from job to job, relationship to relationship. Her parents finally got her to go to a counselor, who diagnosed AD/HD. This knowledge helped her to view herself in a better light, but she still had little confidence in her ability to return to college or to hold down a job. Her relationship pattern was also so deeply ingrained that she didn't know how to meet men without going to a bar or club. And of course, she always ended up with the same type.

For Andrea to change her unhealthy pattern, she first has to do some work on her self-image. Medication may help her cognitive abilities, but repairing her self-esteem will take a lot more time and work.

Spouses and friends may be frustrated by the low self-image of the person with AD/HD. "Why don't you stand up for yourself?" This can have a spiral effect, as the person with AD/HD berates himself for having a poor self-image and then has a *worse* self-image.

Some people overcompensate for a poor self-image by taking unwise risks, by bragging about great achievements (usually some future task that will "turn everything around for us"), or by denying the problems. These traits can also be hard to live with.

The answer, of course, is an honest appraisal of one's situation. Acceptance from spouse and friends is crucial, but they should also encourage the person with AD/HD to see the long, slow path toward healing and renewed confidence. That long-range view is not easy, but along with the proper AD/HD treatment, he or she can embark on that journey.

"DON'T ROCK THE BOAT!"

Earlier we said that people with AD/HD look for change and new challenges. But it is also true that many are resistant to change and don't do well with transitions. We see this with minor changes, such as having to jump from task to task, as in the case of the receptionist who must handle four phone lines at one time. In order to get the job done, some people with AD/HD track tightly into certain tasks and are thrown off when they have to take on a new assignment.

This resistance is also seen with major changes, such as a move to a new home or employment situation. Major moves create so many distractions that people with AD/HD often fear being overwhelmed. Mentally, they can go on "overload" and shut down.

Because many people structure their lives as a way of coping with AD/HD, if someone comes along and disrupts that schedule or routine, it may throw off their whole day. In a work situation, they may ask others to put their requests in writing and to give them prior notice of any changes in their schedule. This may seem cold or arrogant, but in fact, it may be their way of keeping control of their lives.

In the normal give-and-take of most relationships, flexibility is a plus. Flexibility is in short supply for people with AD/HD. This inflexibility can extend to a resistance to dealing with important issues in the relationship (and it might even keep someone from seeking treatment for AD/HD). The person with AD/HD has established certain coping strategies and fears the upheaval of this carefully arranged life. In such cases, a caring friend or spouse can work to replace fear with hope, always remembering that the decision to make positive changes is the responsibility of the one with AD/HD. Others can help, but improving a relationship is a mutual effort. The person with AD/HD needs to take a full share of responsibility.

EIGHT STEPS TO IMPROVE YOUR RELATIONSHIPS

If you have AD/HD, and you want to improve your relationships, what can you do?

One: Seek Treatment

This should go without saying by now, but it's essential. The best thing you can do to improve your relationships is to acknowledge you have a problem with AD/HD and seek treatment for it, through counseling, medication, behavior modification, and/or coaching. You may be amazed at how many other things will fall into place with appropriate treatment.

Two: Accept Yourself

You may have had a history of failure, but that can change. You may have alienated friends, family, or coworkers, but you can now begin to undo some of that damage. You are not doomed to live a life of underachievement and misunderstanding. There is hope for you.

As you begin your journey toward wholeness, involving responsible AD/HD management, it's okay to be where you are. Don't scold yourself for not being two miles up the road. You're here now, and that's fine. You will get there, in time.

Because of AD/HD, you have probably done a lot of things that you aren't proud of. The restoration of your past relationships and/or the building of new relationships requires that you first learn to accept yourself.

Three: Decide to Be Honest

You may have spent a lot of time hiding your problems. Now it's time to open up to the people closest to you. Admit the struggle you have had (and are having) with AD/HD. Ask for help when you need it.

The first ingredient of any good relationship is communication. Communication leads to understanding. You need to explain your situation to the important people in your life. Help them to understand where you've been and where you want to go—with their help.

Four: Give Gifts of Attention

It is expensive to pay attention to other people. Even if medication is helping you to focus, you have a lifetime of distraction that has taught you bad habits. It's still hard work to listen to people, even to your loved ones.

But what if you begin to look at attention as a precious gift you want to give to your spouse or to your children or to your friends? You would spend hard-earned money on flowers or jewelry or expensive video games. Will you spend some attention on these special people? Bring some joy to others by giving them the gift of your undivided attention for specified periods of time.

Five: Practice Active Listening

Listening is a skill that may take some time to learn. Here's one tip: Good listeners are active listeners, not passive listeners. Good listeners get involved in a conversation, prodding the speaker with pertinent questions.

"What happened then?" "How did you feel about that?"

In the past, your mental activity would lead you away from the listening process. Now you need to rechannel your thoughts into words that go back into what the other person is saying. This will take some practice, but it will pay off in more satisfying relationships.

Six: Make Contracts

You may have tended to flit from one thing to another. With proper treatment, you will have less of a need to do that, but you may still have that habit.

It may help to commit to a particular project, hobby, or other pursuit for a period of time. If you take up photography, for instance, decide to stay with it for at least a year. Put regular reminders on your calendar. If you begin to clean up the basement, make a contract with your family in which you (and the others, perhaps) agree to keep working at this project for a month or until it's done, whichever comes first.

If you put these things in writing, it may help to curb your impulsivity. Keep your time commitments short at first and then build them up. Keep your projects at reasonable levels of difficulty with reasonable time frames. Don't expect to re-panel your living room in an hour.

Seven: Establish a System Together

Cooperate with the people you live with and work with, setting up organizational systems that will make life easier for everyone concerned. If you forget things, learn to write them down—even put a blackboard or dry-erase board on the wall so that everyone can be reminded of the tasks and terms agreed to.

If you need regular reminders on certain tasks, ask people for them. Establish with your spouse exactly when reminding becomes "nagging." The third reminder? The eighth? How many reminders do you need?

You may have some systems that you have developed to cope with your AD/HD, but you need to get other people into those systems and set up new systems with them. Most people will be willing to help, as long as they feel that the whole house or office will run more smoothly. A professional coach can also be hired to help you establish and/or maintain a system that works for you.

Eight: Take the Long View

Expect to have setbacks along the way. You will slip into old habits from time to time, and this will disappoint you and the people closest to you. Don't give up hope. This is not a 100-yard sprint, but a marathon. You have plenty of time to pick yourself up and start moving again in the right direction.

It may help to ask others at various intervals, "How am I doing?" Ask them to compare your current behavior to a month ago, or a year ago.

Keep a journal. Even if you only get to it every week or so, it will help you a year from now to see how things were. It will give you bench marks with which to chart your progress as you step steadily toward healing and well-being.

FOR PEOPLE WITHOUT
AD/HD — 7 STEPS TO HELP

If you live with or love someone who has AD/HD and want to help that person change the way he or she interacts in relationships, there are some things you can do, and other things you need to let go of.

1. *Urge the person to get treatment.* You can't do this for the person, but you can help to get information and make some contacts. Without proper treatment, the person with AD/HD is likely to stay in denial and continue the patterns that frustrate you, no matter what you do. Amateur methods are not going to help much. You need professional guidance.

2. *Stop managing the AD/HD for him or her.* Although the following suggestions may seem to contradict this point, it's crucial to develop a certain philosophy of AD/HD management: It is not up to you to manage someone else's AD/HD. You can bend and push and cajole and encourage, but ultimately the person with AD/HD is responsible to deal with his or her problem. If you are constantly covering for someone, the person won't have to develop strategies that work, and you may actually decrease his or her motivation to get help.

3. *Work out a system of organization together.* Set up systems that will help both of you remember what has been said and agreed to. Write things down. Establish places to put certain things, like keys.

4. *Repeat and remind.* Understand that AD/HD creates gaps in the perception of conversations and events. Therefore, you may need to fill in the gaps from time to time. Repeat things without condemnation. Offer cheerful reminders. Give the person with AD/HD a second chance at important information.

5. *Appreciate the expense involved in paying attention.* Keep conversations or information-giving short.

Reward even little bits of attention with love and appreciation. As we have said, it costs someone with AD/HD a lot of energy to pay attention to something or someone for any length of time. If you understand this, it may make you grateful for the attention that is paid and less resentful of the attention that drifts away.

6. *Establish an environment of encouragement.* The person with AD/HD requires patience, as you well know. Often, the surrounding people frequently express judgment, disappointment, and frustration, causing already low self-esteem to sink even lower. The person withdraws all the more, hiding his or her symptoms rather than facing more embarrassment.

Encouragement is a fine art. It involves a lot of stroking, along with occasional kicks in the pants. It says, "I understand your difficulty," and at the same time, "I know you can do better." The person with AD/HD needs to be applauded for efforts to manage and control the problem but also needs to be held accountable for his or her behavior.

Remember that there are some positive aspects of AD/HD that can be affirmed. Is the person creative, forward-thinking, fun to be with? Then say so.

7. *Get your needs met.* People who love someone with AD/HD need to set up healthy boundaries. We hesitate to use the overused term *codependence,* but it can occur in AD/HD situations. You can get so wrapped up in the other person's problem that you ignore your own needs. Communicate these needs to the person with AD/HD. You may be surprised at how these needs get met. On the other hand, he or

she may not be able to meet some of your needs. If not, establish a life of your own, with activities and friends that satisfy these needs. If you love reading books and want to join a book club, you may need to find someone else to share this activity with you.

In any relationship, you need to ask yourself, "What is this relationship about? Is it about me? Is it about the other person? Is it about some problem that he (or she) has or that I have? Or is it about us?" Good relationships are about "us." AD/HD can easily shift the balance in a relationship. You need to do all you can, in love, to shift that balance back.

Just the Facts

► People with AD/HD usually have at least some of the following relational difficulties:
  - Problems in listening to others
  - Impulsively jumping from task to task, or person to person; easily bored
  - Forgetfulness
  - Easily frustrated, leading to angry outbursts
  - Tendency to be self-focused, which can appear selfish
  - Low self-image and insecurity in relationships
  - Difficulty with transitions and change

► These problems can be lessened through communication, honesty, mutual effort, and proper treatment. Both people in a relationship need to understand the problems of AD/HD and allow for a healthy give-and-take of feelings. It's important for those with AD/HD to be held accountable for their actions. Patience, acceptance, and encouragement can go a long way toward helping them make gradual, positive changes in their behavior.

RESOURCES

1. Halverstadt., J., *A.D.D. and Romance: Finding Fulfillment in Love, Sex & Relationships.* Dallas: Taylor Publishing Company, 1998.
2. Novotni, M., *What Does Everybody Else Know That I Don't? Social Skills Help for Adults with AD/HD.* Plantation, FL: Specialty Press, 2001.
3. Solden, Sari, *Women with Attention Deficit Disorder.* Grass Valley, Calif.: Underwood Books, 1995.

▼

CHAPTER EIGHTEEN

WORK

As we consider the experience of the person with AD/HD at work, we're actually encountering two problems at once: learning difficulties and relationship difficulties. The workplace is, of course, a place of learning and doing. The same challenges that a person with AD/HD faces in school can extend to the workplace—blanking out when certain tasks are explained, for instance. But the workplace also has many relationships, and coworkers can have some of the same frustrations about someone with AD/HD that spouses and friends have.

Let's focus on ten particular problems that occur with some frequency among people with AD/HD in the workplace, as well as strategies to help overcome these difficulties.

1. Difficulty with specific tasks
2. The lure of the "other"
3. Missed appointments
4. Impulsive decision-making
5. Rigid patterns
6. The need for a cooperative environment
7. Failure mentality
8. Frustration and anger

9. Ignorance of office politics
10. Hyperactivity

PROBLEM ONE: DIFFICULTY WITH SPECIFIC TASKS

Sometimes people with AD/HD excel at their work. Many of the positive aspects of AD/HD can be harnessed to benefit an employer. But there is a maddening inconsistency—one day you might be a star employee and the next day you're on the ropes.

We have already discussed many of the learning issues that affect the performance of those with AD/HD. Let's briefly examine the major ones here: blinks, time, and transitions.

Sometimes people with AD/HD miss important details of a new assignment. They "blink" while the directions are being given, and so they're not sure how to do a job. Worse, they don't know what they have missed. They think they got it all, but they didn't.

People with AD/HD can take two or three times as long as others to do a project. They tend to be hard workers, and they may put in overtime to get things done, but it takes them longer. They are constantly reviewing what they've read because it didn't stick the first time. Or they have to recalculate a column of numbers because they drifted off.

Transitions are especially challenging. Stopping one thing to start another is a difficult process for those with AD/HD. And yet those transitions may happen many times in a workday. When you have AD/HD, you need extra time to key into a new project.

Marsha was successful in her job, working for a man who probably had AD/HD himself. She answered his phones and typed his letters. Even though he just kept spouting out idea after idea, which tended to drive her crazy, she was able to handle it as long as the business remained small. But then one of his ideas hit it big!

The business took off. New employees were hired. Six phone lines were added, and Marsha was positioned to grow with the company. She and her boss had meetings about profit sharing, stock ownership, and options to purchase future shares. But she felt lost in all of the business growth. Others told her what a great opportunity this was for her, but she longed for the days when it was just a small business with two employees.

Marsha was not able to handle the transitions, the phone calls, and the hectic pace. As new people were added—people who could thrive in such an environment—Marsha couldn't keep up. She gradually lost her place in the pecking order.

Discouraged, frustrated, and feeling left out, she quit her job. While her boss was sad to see her go, he viewed her departure as a necessary loss. He needed to surround himself with people who could handle the pace—those who could follow through on his creative ideas and his hectic schedule.

This story demonstrates two opposite job situations for people with AD/HD. The boss had the freedom to dream and scheme, surrounding himself with people who would deal with the details. His AD/HD may have helped him in his work.

But Marsha was at a level where she had to mind the details. When the business grew, there were too many details. She hit her personal "job ceiling."

This ceiling is an all-too-common reality for those with AD/HD. They see where they want to go, they dream of the possibilities, but they can't get there. Interestingly, it seems that middle management is an especially troublesome swamp for folks with AD/HD. Some people, like Marsha's boss, manage to vault over that whole area. They become executives or entrepreneurs by being in the right place at the right time with the right idea. But others, like Marsha, remain chained to the lower rungs of the corporate ladder. They can do limited tasks very well, but without effective AD/HD treatment, they find it difficult to take on multi-task responsibilities.

PROBLEM TWO: THE LURE OF THE "OTHER"

When you have AD/HD, there's always something else to do. The coffee needs to be made, the paper towels need replenishing, the plants want water. These may all be helpful things to do, but they can keep you from the job at hand. Sometimes it seems that the more important a task is, the more you'll put it off, finding more of those perennial "other things to do."

Remember that people with AD/HD have trouble weighing the importance of tasks—or "executive functioning," as some psychologists call it. Watering the plants can have just as much importance as finishing the annual report, at least in the mind of someone with AD/HD.

With a head full of things to do, you can begin to feel overwhelmed. How do you cope with being overwhelmed? You knock something off the list. Sometimes this happens naturally as a task is simply forgotten. But sometimes the best strategy to get a task done is to cross it off the list. Which task do you cross off? The one that's easiest to do. So you water the plants, because that will only take a minute, rather than working on that report, which you know will take hours.

The only problem is that those "other" tasks always pop up. While you're getting water for the plants, you notice that the sink needs to be washed. While you're getting the paper towels to wash the sink, you see that you're almost out of towels. When you go to the storage cabinet for towels, you see that it's time to order more paper for the photocopier. You may never get to that report.

This is why organizational experts recommend making lists and sticking to them (but not adding new things to the list). Start out with a few minor tasks, they say, but get those done and then focus on your main work. They also suggest breaking down big tasks into small pieces so you can get the same feeling of accomplishment from doing one page of a report as from sharpening all your pencils.

PROBLEM THREE: MISSED APPOINTMENTS

One of the results of AD/HD-related disorganization is chronic lateness or the missing of appointments. In many business settings, this creates huge problems. Employers often assume that the person secretly "wants" to be late or absent, that there is some passive-aggressive rebellion going on. But that is not true at all. The person with AD/HD probably wants to be there on time but honestly forgets or is distracted.

Many missed appointments are simply due to the fact that the person fails to jot down the date and time of the appointment. If you're not attending to the conversation when the appointment is being made, you may lose the details. Even when the arrangements are written down, the paper, calendar, or schedule book is often misplaced.

And even when the appointment is remembered, the schedule book is in hand, and the person with AD/HD is heading out the door, a million distractions await. A rose-bush may need to be smelled, a car may need to be cleaned, shopping may be necessary, an alternate route may suddenly be tempting—and the person arrives a half-hour late with no idea where the time went.

PROBLEM FOUR: IMPULSIVE DECISION-MAKING

Impulsivity can lead to snap decisions, and snap decisions can hurt a company. In chapter 8, we spoke of the man who bought a house one day—just up and bought it—and then told his wife. He was feeling overwhelmed by all the decisions he had to make and he decided to simplify his life by making a bold move. So he bought a house.

But imagine the employee who buys a company car and then tells his boss. Or the one who decides, on a whim, to change computer systems. Or the secretary who decides to put smiley-faces on all the boss's correspondence.

Decision-making is a good thing, especially in business. And there are cases where the impulsivity of a person with AD/HD can come across as a go-getting, take-charge attitude. But a company must also be prepared for those impulsive judgments that are ill-advised. In cases where it would be better to wait awhile, to examine the issues, to test various options, to vent an idea with others in the company, the impulsive person with AD/HD is likely to find trouble.

PROBLEM FIVE: RIGID PATTERNS

Because people with AD/HD are easily distracted, they often develop rigid patterns of action. This seems different from the free-flowing style you might expect, but it's a coping strategy, too. If you lock into a systematic way of doing things, there are fewer distractions.

The problem is, most businesses operate according to Murphy's Law—if things can go wrong, they will. Modern work situations require flexibility to deal with the various curve balls that are thrown. Some people with AD/HD are brilliant at dreaming up new solutions to challenges, but others are locked into their systems and resist change.

PROBLEM SIX: THE NEED FOR A COOPERATIVE ENVIRONMENT

What is your workplace like? Visually, is it stark and bare, or are there posters and calendars up on the walls? What does it sound like? Are there voices gabbing, machines humming, music playing softly in the background or blaring at full volume?

People with AD/HD are greatly affected by their environment. Some cannot tolerate any extraneous noise or movement. If there are people rushing past your desk, you'll be tempted to stop and watch. If there is loud music, you might be drawn away by it.

But the environmental needs are different for everyone. One person with AD/HD needs absolute quiet, another gets more distracted by quiet—his mind keeps imagining what's going on "out there." Some need the comfort of masking noise, anything from canned music to tapes of waves crashing on a rocky beach. Others need the stimulation of bright colors and passersby.

The work environment is an important consideration in any company, but it's especially important for those with AD/HD. If they can get everyone to cooperate in creating the environment they need, they can be effective workers. But in a busy company, such cooperation can be impossible, and the employee will need to work much harder at managing his or her environment.

PROBLEM SEVEN: FAILURE MENTALITY

"Don't define yourself by your challenges or disabilities," says career counselor Wilma Fellman.[1] Some people with AD/HD have had such struggles in life that they assume things will continue to go wrong for them. Their lives have brimmed with great dreams, but again and again they have fallen short of those dreams. Soon they develop a failure mentality; they assume they will not succeed in any new venture.

This can make someone with AD/HD avoid learning situations on the job. While other employees might jump at the chance to take on new responsibilities, a failure-minded person with AD/HD is likely to prefer the same old familiar tasks. This also contributes to rigid patterns, to avoid new ways of doing things.

Imagine the unemployed person who goes out every

▼

day looking for work, only to be rejected. After a while, he or she may give up and stay home. "What's the use?" Some people with AD/HD are in exactly that situation, unemployed and giving up. Others are hanging on to low-level jobs, with dashed hopes of advancement.

This is the depressive side of AD/HD and the reason many are originally diagnosed with depression. They have been so buffeted by a cruel world, a world that always seems a step ahead of them, that they lose their will to succeed. And worst of all, they lose hope.

PROBLEM EIGHT:
FRUSTRATION AND ANGER

Maria tells of times when she would get angry with cowork-ers, or even her boss, and tell them off in no uncertain terms. Now she has learned to anticipate those problems, and she walks away or takes medication or runs six miles.

A person with AD/HD is, in many cases, a simmering pot. All of the frustrations of shattered dreams, missed assign-ments, and failed attempts have been thrown into that pot, and often it boils over.

This is, of course, the flip side of depression. Some people with AD/HD turn the frustration inward and give up hope. Others turn it outward and rage against everyone in their path.

The littlest thing can set them off. They are angry at people who don't understand them. They are angry at the distractions that keep them from working. They are angry at bosses with unreasonable expectations. They are angry at "the system." They are angry at themselves. They are angry at God. And most of all, they are angry at this pain in the neck called Attention Deficit/Hyperactivity Disorder.

Anger is a natural response to a perceived injustice— and there is plenty of injustice perceived by those with AD/HD. They work so hard, and yet it seems they accomplish little. They deserve better.

PROBLEM NINE: IGNORANCE OF OFFICE POLITICS

Life is political—not necessarily in a deceitful, underhanded sense, but in the sense of being aware of office politics. This involves knowing what others want to hear and saying it, recognizing who's in power and granting due respect, and getting the right messages across to the right people at the right time.

All of that takes perception and intuition, an ability to read the subtext of conversations and recognize the cues of body language and seemingly offhand remarks.

Most people with AD/HD don't do that sort of thing. They regularly miss pieces of conversation. They may be extremely perceptive about the pieces they do get, but they're busy trying to reassemble the text of the conversation. They don't have time for subtext.

As a result, people with AD/HD may blurt out inappropriate comments. They may violate unwritten rules. They may offend people without knowing it. They're not being rude; they've just missed out on some of the information that everyone else seems to know.

Offices have politics. So do factories and schools and just about any other workplace. There are unwritten rules everywhere, nuances that people are supposed to "get." But folks with AD/HD can miss out on this whole underworld of information. As a result, it may seem that they don't fit in.

PROBLEM TEN: HYPERACTIVITY

Maria had trouble sitting still for more than ten minutes. If she were in a meeting with her bosses, she would have to get up and walk around after a while. They may have thought that inappropriate, but she had to do it. It was her hyperactivity. If she didn't move, she would burst.

Most office work is based on a simple physical model: People sit at desks and work. But this is unbearable for hyperactive people with AD/HD. They can sit at desks and work for, say, ten minutes, but then they have to stretch their legs. This is one reason why many of the people we have counseled for AD/HD have gone into sales—they have left the confinement of the office to go out on the road where they can move more freely. Or they may start their own business, building in the freedom they require.

But *mental* hyperactivity is also an issue on the job. Workers with AD/HD often find that their minds proceed at a quicker pace than the minds of their coworkers. If someone with AD/HD is running a meeting, he or she may move quickly from point to point without reaching closure on any of the points. The meeting results in much discussion, but no decisions. Other participants in these meetings feel worn out afterward. In a way, they've been introduced to the AD/HD experience—many ideas being juggled at the same time.

Even as participants in meetings, people with AD/HD can come up with brilliant ideas but say them at the wrong times. Alert bosses will jot down these ideas and reintroduce them at the proper time, but many great ideas get lost because no one else was on the same page.

In some cases, hyperactive people with AD/HD are social butterflies. Many are good with people. Their energy makes them fun to be with, and they have fun talking with others. In an office or other workplace, these people can be good for morale. But they can also cut down on office productivity—and not only their own, but also that of the people they talk with.

Again, most of these "social butterflies" don't intend to cheat their companies out of productive hours of labor, but they find a certain amount of success in their social contacts that often eludes them in their desk work. Every time a person walks by, these people with AD/HD are drawn toward a "successful" conversation they might have with that person.

This is another reason why many people with AD/HD thrive in jobs that allow them a great deal of contact with people. They use the positive aspects of their love of socializing rather than fighting the negative aspects of desk work.

How to Succeed in the Workplace

Seek treatment. We know we're sounding like a broken record, but many of the problems cited earlier can be lessened with a proper course of AD/HD treatment, including medication, counseling, behavior modification, and coaching.

Communicate your needs to boss and coworkers. Some people try to hide their AD/HD, but there's no need for that. People around you probably know there's something amiss. You can name it AD/HD or just talk about difficulties with concentration or hyperactivity. If they knew what "it" was, chances are that their response would improve.

It's best not to make demands in the workplace—insisting that they change the environment or ways of doing business just to suit you. But if you present the idea that you want to be a productive worker, and certain changes will increase your productivity for the company, you may get the accommodations without much fuss.

The Americans with Disabilities Act can require companies to make certain accommodations and, if necessary, serves to create a climate in which companies are more apt to make reasonable accommodations than to fire you. If you communicate your needs properly, you may succeed in getting some changes made.

Find your place. There are aspects of AD/HD—creativity, broad thinking, energy—that can make you a very good worker. Other aspects, as we have seen, can create problems. You need to find a job that uses your strengths and minimizes your weaknesses.

This may mean leaving your company and finding a job elsewhere. Or perhaps you can work with the human resources office in your present company to find another niche for you there. Or maybe you can talk with your boss and arrange for different responsibilities.

Set reasonable expectations. Much of the frustration related to AD/HD is a combination of lofty dreams and limited realities. You can see where you want to go—you can see that probably better than most people—but you can't seem to get there.

As you take steps to increase your productivity, you could also take steps to make your dreams more realistic.

Get a sense of what you can reasonably accomplish today, this week, this month. Don't set impossible deadlines or standards you are unlikely to reach. It might help to work with someone else in setting your reasonable goals.

Develop a system of small tasks and immediate rewards. What's the main project you have to do at work right now? How long do you think it will take you to finish? How much of it do you think you can do today? How much can you do in the next hour? What about the next half hour?

Big tasks intimidate a person with AD/HD. That's why so many waste time on trivial little tasks. What's the answer? Making your big task into a series of small tasks. You can decide how small the segments need to be, depending on your usual attention span. But it would not be unreasonable to work on a report one page at a time, or some other assignment a half hour at a time.

When you finish the mini-task, reward yourself in a small way. Get up and take a brief walk. Eat something. Make a phone call. Talk for two minutes with a coworker. Or even water the plants.

Don't let the reward get out of hand, though. Limit the time of the reward to about 10 percent of the time worked. Then plunge back into the next small portion of your main task.

Get the right people around you. If you are a manager or boss, you should be able to hire people whose abilities complement yours. If you aren't, you may still be able to team up with certain employees by letting your boss know whom you work well with.

You need people who are organized and patient. In some cases, these people have limited vision. They don't look at the big picture. That's what you bring to the team. By finding others with complementary skills, you create a synergy that helps everyone work better.

Arrange your work space as best you can. If you have control over where your desk is, what's on the walls, what music is playing, and so on, make the choices that help you work best.

Do you need no distraction, mild (masking) background, or lots of stimulation? You may need to experiment with different arrangements before you find the best one. Ask others to help you with your "testing" of various options. Sometimes people think they know the best conditions to work under, but they're mistaken. Test it out.

Try a buddy system. If you are fortunate enough to have a close friend as a coworker, rely on that friend to fill in some of the gaps for you. You may blurt out inappropriate things without knowing it. You may not hear certain details of an important assignment. You may be spending too much time away from your work station, talking with others. A good friend can help you in all these cases.

Don't be shy about asking for help. Give your friend permission to tell you what you need to hear—even if it's unpleasant. Ask for permission to ask "dumb" questions if you think you missed something. Maybe you could even get regular "How am I doing?" checkups. Be accountable to that person for your behavior on the job. If a supportive coworker or friend isn't available, consider working with a coach or therapist.

You may photocopy pages 268-270 [this section] for your boss or coworkers. Limited permission is granted for this purpose.

WORKING WITH A PERSON
WHO HAS AD/HD

If You're a Boss . . .

Working with someone who has AD/HD can be an exhilarating experience. It can also try your patience. What "reasonable accommodations" can you make in order to bring out the best of what an employee with Attention Deficit/Hyperactivity Disorder has to offer? People with AD/HD tend to be quite creative. Many have a breadth to their thinking that spawns new ideas. That is, they may be in a discussion of marketing strategies, but they're thinking about production and personnel and future planning at the same time. This kind of thinking can create breakthroughs for a company.

But in the daily grind of crunching numbers, filling out forms, and writing reports, they may fall short of expectations. It is not a lack of desire or of intelligence, but a physical difference in the brain that causes inconsistency of attention.

This situation demands understanding and creative solutions. How do you use the pluses of the person with AD/HD while minimizing the minuses? Here are some possibilities.

Rearrange the work space. Talk with the person about the conditions that are best for his or her productivity. Some respond well to busyness and noise; others are easily distracted. We understand that a whole office can't be overhauled for one employee, but reasonable accommodations should be considered. Perhaps moving an office could do the trick, or a change in the background music. Discuss the various options.

Hire complementary personnel. A manager with AD/HD can suggest bold new directions for the business, but will probably not follow through. Can you hire secretaries, assistants, and other managers who will follow through? The person in your office with AD/HD is probably a visionary. You need a detail person to fill the gaps.

Hold structured meetings. A person with AD/HD has trouble structuring his or her own thinking, so it helps when meetings or other communication have structure to them. That is, prepare a written agenda. Number the points. That way, if the employee "blinks" for a minute, he or she will know what was missed.

Repeat and review. It helps if you ask someone with AD/HD to summarize the content of a meeting or the details of an assignment. That way, you'll know if the information got through. If you develop a nonjudgmental spirit with the person, he or she will not try to fake it but will acknowledge parts of the meeting or discussion that were missed. At the end of an important presentation, repeat the main points.

You might also allow the person with AD/HD to tape meetings so the information can be reviewed on his or her own time.

Put things in writing. Write down assignments in detail. It might help to have a note-taker at important meetings who will distribute the notes to those present, including the person with AD/HD. Many with AD/HD find it difficult to take good notes, since they have to split their attention between listening and writing.

Set intermediate deadlines. If you leave people with AD/HD on their own for projects that take six months, they (and you) may be in trouble. Set monthly or biweekly deadlines on an extended project so the employee is accountable on a regular basis.

Find the right responsibilities for the person with AD/HD. There are some tasks that people with AD/HD have great difficulty with—generally detail-oriented paperwork. Of course, many people have difficulty with that, but this is especially true for substantial numbers of those who struggle with AD/HD. They become distracted easily and find it hard to sustain focus. On the other hand, work with creative ideas, work with people, and physically active work can be areas of success for those with AD/HD.

Allow for "exercise breaks." Not all people with AD/HD are hyperactive, but many are. If you have a hyperactive person with AD/HD in your office, you'll know it. It's the person who seems to be walking around the desk more than sitting at it. They pace during meetings or have to leave the room. Or they're always fidgeting.

Those who are diagnosed with AD/HD "with Hyperactivity" just have to move around. It will benefit the company if you encourage regular movement breaks.

Certainly you may come up with other ways to make the best use of your employees with AD/HD, recognizing their distinctive challenges and appreciating their talents. Creativity, flexibility, and patience are crucial.

You may photocopy pages 271-272 [this section] for your coworkers. Limited permission is given for this purpose.

WORKING WITH A PERSON
WHO HAS AD/HD

If You're a Coworker . . .

Working alongside a person with AD/HD can be a challenge, though it also has its rewards. Many of the "reasonable accommodations" listed earlier can be adapted to one-on-one situations. Note especially the point on "Repeat and Review." You may need to go over information a second or third time before the person with AD/HD gets it.

Expect and accept some frustrations. People with AD/HD have to contend with a lot. They usually have big dreams and bigger limitations. They have piled up years of frustration with their own underachievement. That frustration may spill over onto you. In most cases, they're not really mad at you. They're mad at themselves or at their AD/HD. Try to understand their frustration.

Be a buddy. People with AD/HD need people without AD/HD to help them. They need to be able to ask questions about things that you've both just heard or seen. They need people to tell them when they've forgotten something important or said something out of line. You can be that person.

Be considerate, but don't be dominated. You need patience when you're working with a person who has AD/HD. It can be tiring to repeat things, follow through, and make up for the gaps in the person's memory. Sometimes, however, your "patience" can contribute to a sort of codependent relationship.

You need to establish boundaries of just what you will and will not do for the person with AD/HD. When you start to feel used, talk about it and develop new ways of doing things. Those with AD/HD need to be accountable for their own behavior. We hope you can develop a give-and-take arrangement where there is mutual benefit.

Affirm the positive characteristics of the person with AD/HD. Sometimes it seems that the person with AD/HD is intentionally slacking off, not trying to listen, or intentionally being rude. But this is seldom the case. Their brains are not firing exactly right, and occasionally they lose the ability to say no to distraction. In most cases they are trying harder than you know. And in most cases, they deserve applause and respect for coping with their difficulties as well as they have.

People with AD/HD are often energetic and enjoyable. They are often brilliantly creative. Whenever you can, affirm the person for these (and other) positive qualities. Because of the problems they have faced, many with AD/HD have poor self-esteem. They regularly give themselves "You're no good" messages. You can help to counteract those messages by offering sincere praise.

Just the Facts

▶ The workplace may present many difficulties for the adult with AD/HD and for coworkers and bosses, too. The person with AD/HD faces at least ten problem areas at work, including the tendency to "blink" at important moments, to become easily distracted, to start projects but not finish them, and to struggle with personal attitudes and relationships with coworkers.

▶ Effective solutions to these problems are discussed at length on pages 264-267 ("How to Succeed in the Workplace"). They include communicating your needs to your colleagues and making your relationships work for you, working out of your strengths and setting reasonable expectations, breaking down tasks into small pieces, improving your work space, and seeking effective AD/HD treatment.

▶ If you work with someone whose AD/HD is getting in the way, you may be highly frustrated! Pages 268-272 ("If You're a Boss . . ." and "If You're a Coworker . . .") offer suggestions on how to cope as well as how to help.

NOTE

1. Wilma Fellman, *Finding a Career That Works for You* (Plantation, Fla.: Specialty Press, 2000), p. 133.

ADVICE FROM THE TRENCHES

WE HAVE SHARED THE STORIES OF MANY PEOPLE WITH AD/HD, stories with different details and different outcomes. You have met some people who are being treated for AD/HD and some who remain untreated. You have read about the struggles, the failed relationships, the lost jobs, and unrealized dreams. But you have also read about people who have succeeded in overcoming the most crippling aspects of their AD/HD and are enjoying effective, fulfilling lives.

We believe the greatest difference in outcome is due not to the severity of the symptoms but to the attitude of the person with AD/HD.

What does the diagnosis of AD/HD mean to you? It's not a death sentence, not even close. People with AD/HD can live wonderfully exciting and productive lives. We have seen the life-changing effect of proper diagnosis and treatment in the lives of those with AD/HD and in the lives of their families, friends, and colleagues.

AD/HD is not an excuse, a way to duck responsibility. It is a challenge that can be met and overcome. Those who meet the challenge of AD/HD are the ones who succeed.

We asked several people with AD/HD what they would say to someone who isn't sure but thinks he or she might have AD/HD. Here's their advice:

▶ There is no harm in checking it out.

▶ If you think you might have it, pursue it and find out. Not knowing is worse than knowing.

▶ It helped me to know there was a reason for my problems. By taking medication I can now learn anything!

▶ Knowing about AD/HD has hugely affected my self-esteem. There is so much mourning that goes with AD/HD. Find out about it and get on with your life.

▶ It is a disability of sorts, but there is an answer. People should realize it is not merely a matter of attitude or exercise. You have to have help to overcome it.

The next comment comes from Maria Bassler, whose story we told in chapter 9. At the time we were still calling it Attention Deficit Disorder and abbreviating it as ADD. But it's still such a helpful idea that we'll use it as an outline for our final words.

Maria suggested, "Change the acronym for ADD from Attention Deficit Disorder to Accept . . . Do . . . Dream."

ACCEPT

The first step in attitude adjustment is to accept the way we are made: some with AD/HD, some without, and others with some of the symptoms.

Accepting means having your eyes wide open and having accurate information about yourself. You may need to accept that you have AD/HD and learn to face the future with this new knowledge. Acceptance means you are not angry about it, you don't blame others for your problem, and you take full responsibility for your treatment.

On the other hand, you might have to accept that you don't have AD/HD. Facing the truth might involve the realization that you have AD/HD-type symptoms, but that these are due to some other condition such as depression, anxiety, or an overactive thyroid. In either case, it is your responsibility to get the proper treatment.

Do

After you have accepted your diagnosis, do something about it. That usually means seeking treatment! Schedule that appointment you've been putting off, pursue a trial medication, or begin planning the reorganization of your life. You may not want to spend the time or money necessary to make such changes, but these investments are potentially life-changing, not only for you but also for those you love. How else will you know what you might accomplish by taking those first few steps toward change?

When you do something, however, make sure you avoid the impulsive style of the past. Changing jobs, starting a new business, or making a major move is not the kind of decision you want to make without sound advice and caution. Instead, doing something about your condition might mean building into your life a level of accountability that will help you to avoid impulsive, regrettable decisions.

Dream

Now dream your dreams! Once you understand your condition and have taken steps to treat it, there is no reason you can't reach for your dreams. In fact, many people with AD/HD have been quite successful in their endeavors.

What about you? What are your dreams? The only way to start turning your dreams into realities is to take that first step.

"Attitude is a little thing that makes a big difference."

"Accept the challenges of your life so that you may feel the exhilaration of success."

"You become successful the moment you start moving toward a worthwhile goal."

"If one advances confidently in the direction of their dreams, and endeavors to lead a life which they have imagined, they will meet with a success unexpected in common hours."
—Henry David Thoreau

Resources for Adults with AD/HD

Attention Deficit Disorder Association (ADDA)
Formerly the National Attention Deficit
Disorder Association
1788 Second Street, Suite 200
Highland Park, IL 60035
Phone: 847-432-2332
www.add.org

**Children and Adults with Attention Deficit Disorder
(CHADD)**
8181 Professional Place, Suite 201
Landover, MD 20785
Phone: 800-233-4050
www.chadd.org

A.D.D. Ware House
300 Northwest 70th Avenue, Suite 102
Plantation, FL 33317
Phone: 800-233-9273
www.addwarehouse.com

ADDitude Magazine
PO Box 500
Missouri City, TX 77459-9904
Phone: 888-762-8475
www.additudemag.com

The AD/HD Report
Guilford Publications, Inc.
72 Spring Street
New York, NY 10012
Phone: 800-365-7006

ADDvance
1001 Spring Street, Suite 118
Silver Spring, MD 20910
Phone: 888-238-8588
www.addvance.com

Learning Disability Association
4156 Library Road
Pittsburgh, PA 15234
www.ldonline.com

National Association of Professional Organizers
1033 La Posada Drive
Austin, TX 78752
Phone: 512-206-0151

INDEX

rewarding, 106–7, 266
task chunking, 179–80, 216,
        257, 266
time needed for, 102
concentration lapses, 9, 93–94,
        95–96. *See also* blinks;
        inattention
Concerta, 45, 135, 137
connections, 174
Conners Adult Attention Rating
        Scales, 80
consistency, lack of, 94
Continuous Performance Tests
        (CPT), 84
Copeland Symptom Checklist, 80
coping skills. *See also* behaviors;
        structure
    for accommodating person
        with AD/HD, 272
    adaptive behaviors, 85
    adjustment through, 45
    for catching up, 103
    compensatory habits, 64, 204,
        246
    creative, 207–8
    developing, 135
    faking, 23–25
    flexibility and, 244–45
    forgetfulness, 207
    for hyperactivity, 122
    for impulsivity, 116
    for inattention, 113
    interference from, 151, 159
    involving others in, 248
    letting go of, 155
    for missing/incomplete infor-
        mation, 97, 109

respect for, 272
self-medication, 80
counseling, 35, 64, 121, 151–59
    attention deficit management,
        108
    behavioral issues, 163
    for couples, 240
    effectiveness of, 190
    emotional issues, 166
    exploration in, 155
    group therapy, 156–58, 159
    identity issues, 141, 153,
        154–55, 166
    learning problems, 229
    on organizational skills, 204
    referrals for, 66, 67, 68
    relationship issues, 220, 240
    residual issues, 65, 151–53
    role of, 11, 73, 159, 166
    self-esteem issues, 141, 154–55,
        220
    social skills, 152
    stages of, 153–56, 159
    support from, 154–55
    who may provide, 73
courtesy, 176
creativity, 20, 97–98
    in accommodating AD/HD, 270
    applauding, 108
    capitalizing on, 36, 104, 155,
        255, 268
    in coping skills, 207–8
criticism, 173–74
Cylert, 137
daydreaming, 93, 98
deadlines, intermediate, 31, 230,
        270

honesty, 246, 267
hope, 203, 244, 245, 248
　loss of, 261
hyperactivity, 21–23, 26, 54, 119–27
　behavioral, 53
　biofeedback calming, 188–89
　channeling, 113, 122–23, 180
　childhood history of, 121–22, 127
　lack of, 85, 93
　managing, 125–26, 127, 166
　mental, 53, 98, 126, 263
　problems from, 124
　suppressing, 122
　symptoms of, 55, 59, 122,
　　123–24, 127
　in workplace, 254, 263–64
hyperkinesis, 54
hypnosis, 188

identification, 10. *See also* diagnosis
identity, 140, 148, 153, 166. *See
　also* self-esteem
Imipramine, 138
impulsivity, 54, 111–18
　avoiding, 277
　brain activity and, 57–58
　components of, 114–16, 118
　lack of, 85
　managing, 116–17, 118, 138,
　　139, 166, 247
　problems from, 112–13
　in relationships, 233, 236–37
　response delay strategies, 180
　symptoms of, 55, 59
　in work, 253, 258–59
inattention, 54, 59, 93–109. *See
　also* distractions

benefits from, 104–5
blinks. *See* blinks
causes of, 101–2, 132–33
compensating for, 109
components of, 99–100, 109
concentration ability, 98, 202
continuous concentration, 99,
　222
disinhibition. *See* disinhibition
energy cost of paying attention.
　See compensation
　resources
fluctuating, 105, 109, 202
knowledge of missed informa-
　tion, 97, 222, 254, 262–63
learning and, 94–95, 167, 221
mechanisms of, 201
mental activity, 97
organizational difficulties from,
　199–200
overcoming, 106–8, 138
priority and importance of per-
　ceptions, 99, 100, 109,
　206, 256–57
ramifications of, 102–4, 176
reading comprehension,
　94–95
steps in paying attention, 101
symptoms of, 55
to things outside self, 240–41,
　246
time losses from, 104
transitions, 100
types of, 98–99
"weighing" ability, 99, 100,
　109, 206, 256–57
at work, 254

Nortriptyline, 139
note taking, 221, 228, 269
Novotni, Michele, 13, 42
Novotni Social Skills Checklist,
85
NRIs (norepinephrine selective
reuptake inhibitors), 136
nutritional supplementation,
187–88

obligations, 207, 216
observation, powers of, 98–99,
104–5
obsessive/compulsive disorders,
80, 139
oppositional defiant disorder, 79
organization, 19, 199–217
decreasing clutter, 212–13,
216–17
improving, 202–3, 227
inconsistency in, 200–202
of information, 238
learning problems from lack of,
226–27
medications for, 203–4
memory aids, 207, 209, 216,
238, 258
mutual systems, 249
overcoming lack of, 161–62,
167, 175–76
paper handling, 214, 217
planning time, 208–9, 216
of self, 205–10, 216
shopping lists, 214, 217
skills, 204, 215
small steps for, 206–7
of space, 210–12, 216, 267

storage containers, 211, 213,
216, 217
structure and, 178–79, 210–11
of stuff, 212–16, 217
"throwaway budget," 214–15,
217
organizations for adult AD/HD, 72,
146, 279–80
as information resources, 165
overcompensation, 242, 243

pain, 238–39
parents of AD/HD children, 41
passive-aggressiveness, 20, 44
behavior, 32–33
misperception of, 96, 257
patience, 250, 270
Paxil, 135, 139
paying attention. See inattention
people skills, 24, 34, 264
for sales jobs, 19, 36, 161
Perceptin, 140
perceptions
gaps in. See inattention
learning, 152, 262
long-term view, 241–42, 248
priority and importance of, 99,
100, 109, 206, 256–57
perceptions by others, 27
of medication effects, 144–45,
140
of organizational abilities,
200–201
of problem areas, 164
understanding, 233
personality disorders, 80
phenylketonuria, 84

effectiveness of, 134, 190–91
fraudulent, 192
group therapy, 156–58, 159
herbal remedies, 189
for inattention, 109
massage, 190
medication. *See* medications
meditation, 190
mirror treatment, 190
multimodal, 134
nutritional supplementation,
    187–88
options, 86, 157
for other disorders, 47
placebo effect, 193–94
proven, 191
from psychologist, 64
psychosocial, 134
research re, 194–96
self-medication, 24, 80, 239
sensory integration, 190
side effects, 191
testing of, 195
type and order of, 44
variation in, 11, 146
tutors, 228–29
Type A behavior, 123, 124–25,
    127

understanding, 203, 246, 271
urgency, 114, 124
U.S. Department of Education,
    162

vitamins, 188, 191

weaknesses, 35
    compensating for, 21
    minimizing, 265
Wechsler Abbreviated Scale of
    Intelligence (WASI), 82
Wechsler Adult Intelligence Scale
    (WAIS–III), 82
Wellbutrin, 135, 138
Wender Utah Rating Scale, 80
Whiteman, Tom, 13
Woodcock Johnson Tests of Ability
    (WJ–III), 82
work. *See* employment
work skills, 176

yoga, 126
*You Mean I'm Not Lazy, Stupid or
    Crazy?*, 203

Zoloft, 135, 139

AUTHORS

MICHELE NOVOTNI, PH.D., is an expert in the field of AD/HD. She speaks throughout the world on topics related to AD/HD and is the current president of the national Attention Deficit Disorder Association (ADDA). Michele is author of *What Does Everybody Else Know that I Don't? Social Skills Help for Adults with AD/HD*, The *Novotni Social Skills Checklist*, and *Angry with God*. She has appeared on a number of television and radio shows and is a columnist for *ADDitude* magazine. She has also written articles for *Attention*, *FOCUS*, and *ADDvance*. her son, Jarryd, and her father have AD/HD. She is in private practice at the Wayne Counseling Center, Wayne, Pennsylvania. Website *www.michelenovotni.com*.

THOM A. WHITEMAN, PH.D., has dealt extensively with childhood AD/HD and is now a psychologist in private practice specializing in diagnosing and treating adults with AD/HD. He is the founder and president of Life Counseling Services. He is also the president of Fresh Start Seminars, a nonprofit organization that conducts over fifty divorce recovery seminars a year throughout the United States for both adults and children. Dr. Whiteman is the author of eight books.

GET THE HELP YOU DESERVE.